Eat Out! The Outdoor Entertaining Cookbook

Cooking Club
of
America®

MINNETONKA, MINNESOTA

Eat Out! The Outdoor Entertaining Cookbook

Tom Carpenter
Creative Director

Jennifer Guinea
Senior Book Development Coordinator

Shari Gross
Production Coordinator

Laura Belpedio
Senior Book Development Assistant

Rebecca Gammelgaard
Book Design and Production

Bill Lindner
Commissioned Photography

Abigail Wyckoff
Food Stylist

Susan Telleen
Assistant Food Stylist

Peter Conrad
Jason Lund
Photo Assistants

3 4 5 6 7 8 / 06 05 04 03 02

ISBN 1-58159-131-4

Cooking Club of America
12301 Whitewater Drive
Minnetonka, MN 55343

www.cookingclub.com

Special thanks to: Libby Pomroy; Ruth Petran; Bea Krinke; Sarah Anderson; Terry Casey; Denise Bornhausen; Friendly Chevrolet, Fridley, MN; Midway Stadium, St. Paul, MN; Gibbs Farm Museum, Falcon Heights, MN; Minneapolis Farmers' Market, Minneapolis, MN; McCarrons Lake Park, Maplewood, MN; Linder's Greenhouse, St. Paul, MN; and Outdoor Cooking Store, St. Paul, MN.

Contents

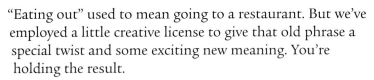

Eating Out

"Eating out" used to mean going to a restaurant. But we've employed a little creative license to give that old phrase a special twist and some exciting new meaning. You're holding the result.

Eat Out! The Outdoor Entertaining Cookbook presents 128 recipes — from the fun and funky to the elegant and exquisite — designed to help you eat and entertain in style when the weather is warm and you can enjoy dining and relaxing outdoors.

Almost everybody loves to eat outside, even if the food was prepared inside. But grilling, and preparing the food outdoors, is often as much a part of the event as the eating itself! This book caters to both fancies, with 25 chapters of menus and selections.

Each menu — such as Steak Dinner, Kansas City Barbecue, Family Picnic, Farmers' Market, No Need to Cook — provides a complete meal idea. You might create the dishes indoors, outdoors, or a combination of both. You'll also find "selections" chapters — such as Pizza on the Grill, Drinks of Summer, Ice Cream Social, Fish on the Grill, Creative Kabobs — that offer an array of summery features to choose from.

Either way, you'll never be short on ideas when you want to entertain *alfresco* or treat your family to a special meal outdoors.

Go on a romantic Picnic for Two, enjoy a traditional Southern-style Celebration, throw a stylish Party for a Crowd, or serve a Fresh & Fabulous Brunch. Or if you're looking for individual ideas to round out some of your own plans, turn to our sections on Summery Salads, Fish on the Grill, Burgers out of the Ordinary, Sandwich Selections and Marinades & More. You can even do a ball game Tailgate Party with class.

Of course, all these meals and dishes are perfect to enjoy outside. But if the weather doesn't quite cooperate or it's just not the right season, rest assured that these recipes will be great indoors too: true tastes of warm weather to brighten any day, savor any time of year.

There you have it. A new plan for "eating out." We think it's a good one, and hope you do too.

Cooking Club
of
America®

MINNETONKA, MINNESOTA

Steak on the Grill

Fourth of July Party

Ice Cream Social

5

pizza
on
the
GRILL

by Patsy Jamieson

*The grill is, simply put,
a wonderful place to make pizza.
Get your entire crew involved!*

Southwestern Chicken Pizza

These aren't your
run-of-the-mill
pizza recipes, no way.
The ideas, the ingredients,
the grill ... hey, pizza is fun
(and a delight to eat) again!

Southwestern Chicken Pizza

A cornmeal crust makes a great platform for a Southwestern-flavored stir-fry of chicken and peppers. Monterey Jack cheese finishes off this pizza. For optimum freshness and to be sure that the topping is hot, make the chicken topping just before grilling the pizzas.

1	recipe *Cornmeal Pizza Crust* (page 17)	¼	teaspoon salt
2	cups (8 oz.) grated Monterey Jack cheese	¼	teaspoon freshly ground pepper
		1	medium onion, slivered
1	cup chopped fresh cilantro	1	medium red bell pepper, seeded, diced
3	tablespoons extra-virgin olive oil		
	Cornmeal for dusting	3	garlic cloves, minced
12	oz. boneless skinless chicken breast halves, sliced	1¼	cups salsa

1. Prepare Cornmeal Pizza Crust.

2. While pizza dough is resting, set cheese, cilantro and 2 tablespoons of the oil on tray. In addition, place the following equipment on the tray: pastry brush, tongs, wide metal spatula, small off-set metal spatula or blunt knife for spreading rubber spatula, large spoon and measuring cups.

3. Dust 2 baking sheets with cornmeal. Divide pizza dough into 4 pieces. On lightly floured surface, roll each piece into 9-inch round crust about ⅛ inch thick. (Keep pieces of dough covered when you are not working with them.) Place crusts on baking sheets. Cover and refrigerate until needed.

4. Prepare grill for indirect cooking. (See *Preparing a Grill for Pizza*, page 12.)

5. Season chicken with salt and pepper. In large nonstick skillet, heat remaining 1 tablespoon of the oil over medium-high heat. Add chicken; cook 3 to 4 minutes, stirring often, or until lightly browned and no longer pink in center. Transfer to plate. Add onion, bell pepper and garlic to skillet; sauté 3 to 5 minutes, stirring often, or until just tender. Add salsa; bring to a simmer, stirring constantly. Stir in reserved chicken. Transfer to bowl. Add to tray with prepared toppings and equipment.

6. Lift one crust with your hands and drape over hotter part of grill. Repeat with second crust. Cover grill. Cook crusts 1 to 1½ minutes or until puffed and grill marks appear on underside. Using tongs, flip crusts over onto cooler part of grill. Working quickly, brush each crust lightly with oil. Spread about 1 cup chicken mixture over each crust. Top with about ½ cup cheese. Cover grill and cook pizzas 2 to 3 minutes or until bottom crusts are crisp and cheese begins to melt. Using wide metal spatula, transfer pizzas to individual plates. Garnish each pizza with sprinkling of cilantro. Serve immediately. Meanwhile, repeat with remaining crusts and toppings.

4 servings

Grilled Pizza with Pesto and Tomatoes

This is the ultimate summer pizza. It features a simple topping of pesto and juicy, ripe tomatoes. Served over a crisp grilled crust, it can't be beat.

1 recipe *Cornmeal Pizza Crust* (page 17)	¼ teaspoon salt
1 recipe Pesto (see below)	½ cup torn fresh basil
3 tomatoes, diced, seeded	¼ cup pine nuts, toasted*
3 tablespoons extra-virgin olive oil	Cornmeal for dusting

TIP:

*To toast pine nuts, heat pine nuts over medium-low heat in small skillet, stirring constantly, 3 to 4 minutes or until light golden and fragrant. Transfer to small bowl and let cool.

1. Prepare Cornmeal Pizza Crust.

2. While pizza dough is resting, prepare Pesto.

3. In medium bowl, toss tomatoes with 1 tablespoon of the oil and salt. Set on tray, along with fresh basil, pine nuts, Pesto and remaining 2 tablespoons oil. In addition, place following equipment on tray: pastry brush, tongs, rubber spatula, small offset metal spatula or blunt knife for spreading, large metal spatula, large spoon and measuring cups.

4. Prepare grill for indirect cooking (See *Preparing a Grill for Pizza*, page 12.)

5. Dust 2 baking sheets with cornmeal. Divide pizza dough into 4 pieces. On lightly floured surface, roll each piece into 9-inch round crust about ⅛ inch thick. (Keep pieces of dough covered when you are not working with them.) Place crusts on baking sheets.

6. Lift one crust with your hands and drape over hotter part of grill. Repeat with second crust. Cover grill and cook crusts 1 to 1½ minutes or until puffed and grill marks appear on underside. Using tongs, flip crusts over onto cooler part of grill. Working quickly, brush each crust lightly with oil. Spread about ⅓ cup Pesto over each crust. Sprinkle with about ¾ cup tomatoes. Cover grill and cook 3 to 5 minutes or until bottoms are crisp and toppings are heated through. Using wide metal spatula, transfer pizzas to individual plates. Garnish each pizza with basil and pine nuts. Serve immediately. Meanwhile, repeat with remaining crusts and toppings.

4 individual pizzas

Pesto

The easiest way to preserve fresh basil is simply to make up a batch of *Pesto*. Keep it on hand for summer pizza and pasta dishes (like *Grilled Pizza with Pesto and Tomatoes*), or freeze so you can enjoy the taste of summer during cooler months.

4 cups chopped fresh basil	½ teaspoon freshly ground pepper
½ cup pine nuts, toasted*	¼ cup extra-virgin olive oil
3 garlic cloves, minced	¾ cup (3 oz.) freshly grated
½ teaspoon salt	Parmesan cheese

1. In food processor, process basil, pine nuts, garlic, salt and pepper until pine nuts are ground. With motor running, gradually add oil; process until paste forms. Add cheese; pulse until blended. Transfer to bowl.

2. Place sheet of plastic wrap directly on surface. Refrigerate mixture up to 2 days or freeze up to 3 months. Thaw in refrigerator. Bring to room temperature before spreading over pizza crust.

1⅓ cups

Grilled B.L.T. Pizza

This pizza takes the much-loved sandwich combination of bacon, lettuce and tomatoes to a new level. If, because of health concerns, it has been a while since you have enjoyed bacon, try this pizza with lower-fat bacon or turkey bacon. Both options are available in supermarkets.

1	recipe *Whole Wheat Pizza Crust* (page 17)	¼	teaspoon freshly ground pepper
8	oz. thick-sliced bacon, cooked, cut into 1-inch pieces	3	cups shredded romaine lettuce
3	tomatoes, diced, seeded	3	tablespoons extra-virgin olive oil
¼	teaspoon salt	3	cups (12 oz.) grated sharp cheddar cheese
			Cornmeal for dusting

1. Prepare Whole Wheat Pizza Crust.

2. While pizza dough is resting, in medium bowl, toss tomatoes with salt and pepper. Place on tray. Place lettuce in large bowl and place on tray, along with oil and cheese. In addition, place the following equipment on tray: pastry brush, tongs, wide metal spatula, large spoon and measuring cups.

3. Prepare grill for indirect cooking. (See *Preparing a Grill for Pizza*, page 12.)

4. Dust 2 baking sheets with cornmeal. Divide pizza dough into 4 pieces. On lightly floured surface, roll each piece into 9-inch round crust about ⅛ inch thick. (Keep pieces of dough covered when you are not working with them.) Place crusts on prepared baking sheets.

5. Lift one crust with your hands and drape over hotter part of grill. Repeat with second crust. Cover grill and cook crusts 1 to 1½ minutes or until puffed and grill marks appear on underside. Using tongs, flip crusts over onto cooler part of grill. Working quickly, brush each crust lightly with oil. Sprinkle about ¾ cup cheese over each crust. Top with about ¼ cup bacon and about ¾ cup tomatoes. Cover grill and cook pizzas 2 to 3 minutes or until bottoms are crisp and toppings are heated through. Using wide metal spatula, transfer pizzas to individual plates. While pizzas are cooking, toss romaine with 1 tablespoon of the oil. Garnish each pizza with mound of romaine. Serve immediately. Meanwhile, repeat with remaining crusts and toppings.

4 individual pizzas

Grilled Pizza with Caramelized Onions, Goat Cheese and Arugula

Preparing a Grill for Pizza

SUCCESSFUL GRILLED PIZZA USES THE INDIRECT GRILLING METHOD.

- If using a gas grill, heat all burners on high until temperature reaches between 500°F and 550°F. This will take 10 to 15 minutes. Just before cooking, turn off one of the burners so that there is no direct heat under one part of the grill. (If your grill has 3 burners, turn off the center burner.)

- If using a charcoal grill, light charcoal and let burn until covered with thin layer of gray ash. This will take about 30 minutes. (Note: Timing in the accompanying grilled pizza recipes is based upon using a gas grill. If using a charcoal grill, you will need to prepare the grill earlier than stated in recipe.) Using long grill tongs, divide coals into 2 piles on either side of grill, leaving an area in center of grill where there is no direct heat.

- Grilled pizzas cook very quickly, so you need to be well organized before you start cooking. You will need a convenient surface near the outdoor grill for holding crusts, toppings and equipment. Supplement your outdoor work space with portable tables, if necessary. Assemble and double check pizza toppings and equipment before heading out to the grill.

Grilled Pizza with Caramelized Onions, Goat Cheese and Arugula

This grilled pizza will please sophisticated palates. A garnish of peppery arugula salad makes a pleasing contrast to the flavorful caramelized onion-and-goat cheese topping.

PIZZA

3 tablespoons extra-virgin olive oil
2 medium to large sweet
    onions, sliced
½ teaspoon salt
1 recipe *Whole Wheat Pizza Crust*
    (page 17)
1⅓ cups (about 6 oz.) crumbled
    goat cheese
2 medium tomatoes,
    diced, seeded
    Cornmeal for dusting

SALAD

2 tablespoons extra-virgin olive oil
1 tablespoon balsamic vinegar
¼ teaspoon salt
⅛ teaspoon freshly ground pepper
6 cups torn arugula

1. In large skillet, heat 1 tablespoon of the oil over medium heat until hot. Sauté onions and salt 15 to 20 minutes or until very tender and lightly browned. Adjust heat as necessary and add a little water if needed, to prevent scorching. Transfer to medium bowl. (Caramelized onions can be stored, covered, in the refrigerator up to 2 days. Bring to room temperature before spreading over pizza crust.)

2. Prepare Whole Wheat Pizza Crust.

3. While pizza dough is resting, set goat cheese, tomatoes, remaining 2 tablespoons of the oil and caramelized onions on tray. In addition, place the following equipment on tray: pastry brush, tongs, wide metal spatula, small off-set metal spatula or blunt knife for spreading, rubber spatula, large spoon, measuring cups, salad spoon and fork.

4. To prepare salad: In small bowl or jar, combine 2 tablespoons oil, vinegar, salt and pepper; whisk or shake to mix. Place arugula in large bowl. Set dressing and arugula on tray with toppings and equipment.

5. Prepare grill for indirect cooking. (See *Preparing a Grill for Pizza*, page 12.)

6. Dust 2 baking sheets with cornmeal. Divide pizza dough into 4 pieces. On lightly floured surface, roll each piece into 9-inch round crust, about ⅛ inch thick. (Keep pieces of dough covered when you are not working with them.) Place crusts on baking sheets.

7. Lift one crust with your hands and drape dough over hotter part of grill. Repeat with second crust. Cover grill and cook crusts 1 to 1½ minutes or until puffed and grill marks appear on underside. Using tongs, flip crusts over onto cooler part of grill. Working quickly, brush each crust lightly with oil. Spread about ⅓ cup caramelized onions over each crust. Sprinkle with about ⅓ cup cheese and about ½ cup tomatoes. Cover grill. Cook pizzas 2 to 3 minutes or until bottoms are crisp and toppings are heated through. Using wide spatula, transfer pizzas to individual plates. While pizzas are cooking, toss arugula with dressing. Garnish each pizza with mound of salad. Serve immediately. Meanwhile, repeat with remaining crusts and toppings.

4 servings

Grilled Pizza Margherita

Grilled Pizza Margherita

In the world of grilled pizza, simplicity reigns. This classic Pizza Margherita—made with good tomato sauce, fresh mozzarella and a garnish of fresh basil—is well suited to grilling and makes a perfect hot weather meal.

1	recipe *Summer Tomato Sauce* (page 17)	3	tablespoons olive oil
1	recipe *Quick Pizza Crust* (page 17)	¾	cup chopped fresh basil
8	oz. fresh mozzarella cheese, drained	⅛	teaspoon freshly ground pepper
			Cornmeal for dusting

1. Prepare Summer Tomato Sauce.

2. Prepare Quick Pizza Crust.

3. While pizza dough is resting, cut mozzarella into ¼-inch-thick slices. Lay slices out on a plate; pat dry with paper towels. Set on tray, along with oil, basil leaves, a pepper mill and Summer Tomato Sauce. In addition, place the following equipment on the tray: pastry brush, tongs, wide metal spatula, small off-set metal spatula or blunt knife for spreading, rubber spatula, large spoon and measuring cups.

4. Prepare grill for indirect cooking. (See *Preparing a Grill for Pizza*, page 12.)

5. Dust 2 baking sheets with cornmeal. Divide pizza dough into 4 pieces. On lightly floured surface, roll each piece into 9-inch round crust about ⅛-inch thick. (Keep pieces of dough covered when you are not working with them.) Place crusts on prepared baking sheets.

6. Lift one crust with your hands and drape over hotter part of grill. Repeat with second crust. Cover grill and cook crusts 1 to 1½ minutes or until puffed and grill marks appear on underside. Using tongs, flip crusts over onto cooler part of grill. Working quickly, brush each crust lightly with oil. Spread about ⅓ cup tomato sauce over each crust. Top with slices of cheese. Cover grill. Cook pizzas 2 to 3 minutes or until bottoms are crisp and cheese begins to melt. Using a wide metal spatula, transfer pizzas to individual plates. Garnish each pizza with basil, a drizzle of oil and pepper. Serve immediately. Meanwhile, repeat with remaining crusts and toppings.

4 servings

Grilled Pizza with Potato-Rosemary Topping

The state of Oaxaca in Mexico is a mecca to food enthusiasts. Oaxacan food is extraordinary, but on a recent trip to this magical area, my surprise discovery was some of the best pizza I have ever tasted. At the cozy restaurant Pizzeria Nostrana in the capital, Oaxaca City, I enjoyed an incredible pizza with a delicate potato-rosemary topping. When I returned home, I was determined to adapt the idea to an American home kitchen. Here is the version I've worked out using an outdoor grill.

1 recipe *Summer Tomato Sauce* (page 17)	4 teaspoons chopped fresh rosemary
1 recipe *Quick Pizza Crust* (page 17)	1 teaspoon salt
4 to 6 Yukon Gold potatoes, peeled	½ teaspoon freshly ground pepper
Cooking spray	3 cups (12 oz.) freshly grated
4 teaspoons plus 2 tablespoons olive oil	mozzarella cheese*

TIP:

*Do not use fresh mozzarella for this recipe. Fresh cheese has a high moisture content and may make the pizzas soggy.

TIP:

**To ensure uniformly thin potato slices, use a food processor fitted with a thin (2 mm) slicing disc or a mandolin-style manual vegetable slicer.

1. Prepare Summer Tomato Sauce.

2. Prepare Pizza Crust.

3. While pizza dough is resting, prepare grill for indirect cooking. (See *Preparing a Grill for Pizza*, page 12.)

4. Slice potatoes ⅛-inch thick.** Place 22-inch sheet aluminum foil on counter. Spray with cooking spray. Arrange ¼ of the potatoes, slightly overlapping, in 7½-inch circle in center of sheet. Drizzle 1 teaspoon oil over potatoes. Sprinkle with 1 teaspoon rosemary, ¼ teaspoon salt and ⅛ teaspoon pepper. Bring short edges of foil together and fold over several times. Pinch and fold ends together to seal packet. Make second packet. Place 2 packets on cooler part of grill. Cover grill and cook packets 12 to 15 minutes or until potatoes are tender. (You will have to open packet to check doneness. Be careful of steam.) While packets are cooking, make an additional 2 packets with remaining potatoes. When all packets are cooked, set aside near grill.

5. Set cheese, remaining 2 tablespoons oil and Tomato Sauce on tray. In addition, place following equipment on tray: pastry brush, tongs, wide metal spatula, small off-set metal spatula or blunt knife for spreading, rubber spatula, large spoon and measuring cups.

6. Dust 2 baking sheets with cornmeal. Divide pizza dough into 4 pieces. On lightly floured surface, roll each piece into 9-inch round crust about ⅛-inch thick. (Keep pieces of dough covered when you are not working with them.) Place crusts on prepared baking sheets.

7. Open potato packets; slide a wide metal spatula under potato cakes to loosen. Lift a crust with your hands and drape over hotter part of the grill. Repeat with second crust. Cover grill and cook crusts 1 to 1½ minutes or until puffed and grill marks appear on the underside. Using tongs, flip crusts over onto cooler part of grill. Working quickly, brush each crust lightly with oil. Spread about ⅓ cup tomato sauce over each crust. Sprinkle with about ¾ cup cheese. Using a wide metal spatula, transfer potato cake to top of each pizza. Cover grill. Cook pizzas 2 to 3 minutes or until bottoms are crisp and toppings are heated through. Using wide metal spatula, transfer pizzas to individual plates. Serve immediately. Meanwhile, repeat with remaining crusts and toppings.

4 servings

Summer Tomato Sauce

Here is a super-simple, all-purpose tomato sauce to help you take advantage of tomatoes while they are at their peak. When time is short, I bypass the step of peeling the tomatoes, but if you prefer a less rustic sauce, peel the tomatoes before dicing. Drop them into boiling water for a few seconds to loosen skins before peeling. When tomatoes are not in season, substitute 3 (14-oz.) cans diced tomatoes for fresh tomatoes.

1	tablespoon olive oil	¼	teaspoon salt
4	garlic cloves, minced	¼	teaspoon freshly ground pepper
⅛	teaspoon crushed red pepper		
5	medium ripe tomatoes, diced, seeded		

1. In large saucepan, heat oil over medium-low heat until warm. Sauté garlic and crushed red pepper 30 to 60 seconds, stirring constantly, until softened and fragrant but not colored.

2. Stir in tomatoes and salt. Increase heat to medium-high and bring to a simmer.

3. Reduce heat to medium-low. Simmer, uncovered, 25 to 30 minutes. Stir often until tomatoes have broken down and thickened. Season with freshly ground pepper. (The sauce will keep, covered, in the refrigerator up to 4 days or in the freezer up to 3 months. Warm on stovetop or in microwave before using.)

1 ¾ cups

Quick Pizza Crust

An outdoor grill turns any amateur pizza maker into a master pizza chef because it ensures an incredibly crisp, light result. And what's more, homemade pizza dough is fast and easy to make. Quick-rising yeast shortens rising time to 10 minutes and a food processor accomplishes the mixing and kneading process in just a few minutes.

2	cups all-purpose flour	⅔	cup hot water (120°F to125°F)*
1	(¼-oz.) pkg. quick-rising yeast	1	tablespoon olive oil
1	teaspoon salt		Cooking spray
½	teaspoon granulated sugar		

1. In food processor, combine flour, yeast, salt and sugar; pulse to mix. In measuring cup, combine hot water and oil. With motor running, gradually add hot liquid to processor; process until dough forms ball. Process an additional 1 minute to knead. The dough should be quite soft. If it seems dry, add 1 to 2 tablespoons warm water; if too sticky, add 1 to 2 tablespoons flour.

2. Transfer dough to lightly floured surface. Spray sheet of plastic wrap with cooking spray and place, sprayed-side down, over dough. Let dough rest 10 to 20 minutes. (Dough can prepared ahead, enclosed in resealable plastic bag and refrigerated overnight. Bring to room temperature before using.) Proceed as directed in pizza recipe.

crust for 4 individual pizzas

TIP:

*Quick-rising yeast requires hotter water than standard yeast. Use an instant-read thermometer to check temperature of hot tap water. Heat in microwave or on stovetop, if necessary.

WHOLE WHEAT PIZZA CRUST
Substitute 1 cup whole wheat flour for 1 cup all-purpose flour.

CORNMEAL PIZZA CRUST
Substitute ½ cup cornmeal for ½ cup all-purpose flour.

Drinks of Summer

by Beatrice Ojakangas

This inspiring arsenal of summer drink ideas will, no doubt, keep you and your guests cool and happy.

Apple-Orange Julius

Chocolate
Cappuccino Float

Coconut Colada Punch

Mock
Champagne Punch

Raspberry
Campari Punch
by the Pitcher

Lemon Gingerade

Mango, Banana and
Strawberry Smoothie

Orange-Tomato
Cocktail

Apple-Orange Julius

Fruits dominate the ingredient lists in this line-up of summer drink selections. Pick and choose the drinks you want for different occasions.

Apple-Orange Julius

Serve this refreshing drink for breakfast or brunch, or as a snack on a steaming hot day!

1 (6-oz.) can frozen orange juice concentrate, thawed
1 (6-oz.) can frozen apple juice concentrate, thawed
⅓ cup instant nonfat dry milk

¼ cup powdered sugar
1 teaspoon vanilla
2 trays ice cubes (about 24 cubes)
3 cups water

1. In blender, combine orange and apple juice concentrates, dry milk, powdered sugar, vanilla and ice cubes. Add 1 cup of the water; blend at high speed until smooth and frothy. Add remaining water while processing (or if all of the water will not fit into the container, pour into large pitcher and whisk in remaining water). Garnish each drink with orange slices.

8 (8-oz.) servings

Chocolate Cappuccino Float

This icy version of the favorite Italian-style coffee is refreshing on a hot day. To turn it into a dessert drink, add one or two tablespoons of Kahlua to the coffee before adding ice cream.

¾ cup brewed espresso coffee, chilled
⅓ cup vanilla ice milk or ice cream*

2 tablespoons whipped cream
½ teaspoon sweetened cocoa powder

1. Pour coffee into 1 (10-oz.) chilled glass. Top with ice cream and dollop of whipped cream. Dust with cocoa powder.

1 (8-oz.) serving

TIP:
*A #12 ice cream scoop measures ⅓ cup ice cream.

Coconut Colada Punch

Here's the perfect punch to serve for a shower in the summertime, or to complement a tropical buffet menu.

1 (15-oz.) can cream of coconut
1 (46-oz.) can frozen pineapple juice concentrate, thawed
1 quart ice cubes

1 liter club soda, chilled

1. In large, chilled punch bowl or pitcher, whisk together cream of coconut and pineapple juice. Add ice cubes and sparkling water just before serving. Garnish with mint leaves.

18 (6-oz.) servings

Raspberry Campari Punch by the Pitcher

Mock Champagne Punch

This is a perfect punch to serve for a summertime shower or wedding reception. It can be made entirely alcohol-free, if desired. To retain the bubbly character, put the punch together just before serving. But you need to make the ice ring at least 24 hours in advance.

ICE RING (optional)
1   quart white grape juice
1   cup fresh strawberries

PUNCH
1   liter chilled club soda
1   liter chilled ginger ale
1   quart white wine or
        white grape juice
2   (12-oz.) bottles pale ale
        or near beer

1. Prepare ice ring one day ahead.

2. Pour small amount of grape juice into 5- to 6-cup ring mold; place in freezer until frozen. Place strawberries on top of frozen layer; pour in grape juice until strawberries are partially submerged. Freeze to fix berries into ring. Pour in remaining grape juice to fill ring; freeze until solid.

3. To serve, unmold ice ring into chilled punch bowl. Pour in club soda, ginger ale, white grape juice and beer. Serve immediately.

20 (6-oz.) servings

Raspberry Campari Punch by the Pitcher

Campari, the popular bitter Italian apertif, has an astringent, bittersweet flavor and a pretty pink color. It is often mixed with soda and served over ice. Here we mix Campari with raspberry-cranberry juice to cut the alcoholic content considerably without sacrificing flavor.

1   (11.5-oz.) can frozen
        cranberry-raspberry
        juice concentrate, thawed

1   (750 ml) bottle mineral water, chilled
1   cup Campari, chilled

1. Combine cranberry-raspberry juice concentrate, mineral water and Campari in pitcher; chill. Fill glasses with 2 to 3 ice cubes each and pour Campari mixture over ice. Garnish each serving with two or three fresh raspberries.

6 (7½-oz.) servings

Lemon Gingerade

Keep this refreshing, slightly spicy version of lemonade on hand in your refrigerator for a delightful pick-me-up in the middle of a hot afternoon.

4 lemons	1 gallon cold water
1 (4-oz.) piece fresh ginger	1 (12-oz.) bottle honey

1. Scrub lemons thoroughly and cut in half crosswise. Wash ginger in hot water; scrape off skin. Cut into paper-thin slices.

2. In Dutch oven, combine water and ginger slices. Squeeze lemons; add pulp, juice and lemon halves to pot. Bring to a boil over medium-high heat. Remove from heat, cover and steep 30 minutes.

3. Strain through fine-mesh strainer while still hot; stir in honey. Cool, then refrigerate. Serve over ice; garnish with mint sprigs.

16 (8-oz.) servings

Mango, Banana and Strawberry Smoothie

Frozen bananas and strawberries are the key to making this frosty smoothie thicker and colder. You can buy fruit already frozen, or freeze your favorite fruit yourself (see note).

1 cup diced fresh mango	6 to 8 ice cubes
1 cup sliced fresh bananas	½ cup vanilla yogurt or
1½ cups fresh strawberries	vanilla-flavored soy milk
1 cup fresh orange juice	

1. In blender, combine mango, banana slices, strawberries, orange juice, ice cubes and yogurt at high speed; process until smooth.

4 (8-oz.) servings

Note:

Cut ripe bananas into bite-size pieces and freeze in a single layer; once frozen, place in a resealable plastic bag for smoothie-making. One banana equals about 1 cup of slices.

Orange-Tomato Cocktail

Tomato juice puts a rosy blush on orange juice. The result? A refreshing, not-too-sweet cocktail that's perfect for brunch, as well as before dinner, with or without the "spike."

2 cups fresh orange juice, chilled	4 tablespoons (2 oz.) tequila or
1 cup fresh tomato juice, chilled	vodka, if desired
2 tablespoons fresh lime juice	2 drops hot pepper sauce

1. Combine orange juice, tomato juice, lime juice, tequila and hot pepper sauce in pitcher. Pour over ice cubes in four tall glasses. Garnish with celery stick and lime wedges.

4 (6-oz.) servings

Lemon Gingerade

Mango, Banana and Strawberry Smoothie

Picnic
for Two

by Mary Evans

When the picnic gathering is intimate and romantic, this menu offers sophisticated fare befitting of the occasion.

menu

Garlic-Rubbed Beef Tenderloin Slices with Sun-Dried Tomato Tapenade

Goat Cheese, Roasted Pepper and Pine Nut Pâté

Pesto and Green Bean Potato Salad

Chocolate-Almond Mousse

Garlic-Rubbed Beef Tenderloin Slices with Sun-Dried Tomato Tapenade

From tenderloin with tapenade to an unbelievable mousse, this isn't your standard picnic fare. But that's what makes this menu extra special.

Garlic-Rubbed Beef Tenderloin Slices with Sun-Dried Tomato Tapenade

When roasting small pieces of meat, it's good to remember that the cooking time per pound of meat increases significantly over a larger piece. Use an instant-read thermometer to check for desired doneness.

TENDERLOIN
- 1 teaspoon minced garlic
- ¼ teaspoon salt
- 1 teaspoon olive oil
- ¼ teaspoon freshly ground pepper
- 1 (10-oz.) beef tenderloin

TAPENADE
- 2 tablespoons chopped sun-dried tomatoes packed in oil, drained
- 1 tablespoon chopped kalamata olives
- 2 teaspoons chopped fresh oregano
- 2 teaspoons chopped capers
- 1 teaspoon Worcestershire sauce

Note:

Let the tenderloin rest before refrigerating — this allows all the juices to distribute evenly through the interior and gives an even pink color to the meat when sliced. Remember to slice the meat before packing your picnic basket. Add a sealed ice block to keep everything chilled en route.

1. Heat oven to 400°F.

2. Mash garlic with salt on cutting board using back of fork to form paste; blend together with olive oil and pepper in small bowl. Rub over beef; let stand 15 minutes.

3. Roast tenderloin 25 to 35 minutes or until internal temperature reaches 160°F. Let rest 30 minutes. Refrigerate, wrapped in plastic wrap, until cold.

4. Finely chop sun-dried tomatoes, olives, oregano and capers to rough paste. In small bowl, combine paste and Worcestershire sauce. Refrigerate, covered, until ready to serve.

5. Serve thinly sliced beef on sliced foccacia or French bread topped with dollop of tapenade.

2 servings, ¼ cup tapenade

Goat Cheese, Roasted Pepper and Pine Nut Pâté

Shape this pretty spread into a log using a sheet of plastic wrap. Make layers on top of the wrap, as directed, then roll into a log using the plastic wrap as a guide.

- ½ red bell pepper, halved, seeded
- 1 tablespoon pine nuts

- 1 (3.5- to 4-oz.) pkg. Montrachet or other goat cheese
- 1 tablespoon chopped fresh thyme

1. Heat broiler.

2. Place bell peppers skin side up on baking sheet. Broil 3 to 4 minutes or until skin blackens. Let cool and remove skin. Chop into ¼-inch pieces; set aside.

3. Heat small skillet over medium-high heat until hot. Toast pine nuts, stirring often, 1 to 2 minutes or until light brown. Remove to small bowl; let cool.

4. Crumble goat cheese into small bowl; toss with thyme. Line 4½- x2½-inch loaf pan with plastic wrap, allowing small overhang.

5. Sprinkle pine nuts over bottom of pan. Sprinkle ¼ of the goat cheese over pine nuts. Sprinkle ⅓ of the bell pepper pieces over goat cheese; repeat with ¼ of the goat cheese and ⅓ bell pepper pieces. Continue layering, finishing with remaining ¼ the goat cheese.

6. Wrap overhanging plastic wrap over top. Press gently but firmly on top to seal layers together. Refrigerate until ready to serve; unmold. Serve with crackers or thinly sliced French bread.

2 servings = 1 cup

Pesto and Green Bean Potato Salad

Purchase pesto in the refrigerated section of your grocery store. Keep it on hand to toss with pasta or stir into your spaghetti sauce for a flavor boost.

¼	lb. red potatoes, quartered	2	tablespoons pesto
⅛	teaspoon salt	1½	teaspoons extra-virgin olive oil
1	cup water	1	teaspoon white wine vinegar or
¼	lb. green beans, cut into		cider vinegar
	1-inch pieces	¼	teaspoon lemon pepper

1. In medium saucepan, cover potatoes with lightly salted water. Bring to a boil over medium-high heat; cook about 20 minutes or until fork-tender. Drain; cool.

2. Bring 1 cup water to a boil in small saucepan over medium heat. Cook green beans 5 to 8 minutes or until tender. Drain.

3. Cut potatoes into bite-size pieces. Combine potatoes with green beans in medium bowl. In small bowl, whisk together pesto, oil, vinegar and lemon pepper; pour over potatoes. Toss to coat. Refrigerate, covered, until ready to serve.

2 servings

Chocolate-Almond Mousse

This simple-to-prepare mousse tastes like you spent hours preparing it. Pack the mousse straight from the freezer—it will thaw while you enjoy the rest of the picnic. By the time you're ready for dessert, the mousse is too!

5	tablespoons heavy cream	½	cup semisweet chocolate chips (6 oz.)
4	teaspoons almond-flavored liqueur	1	(3-oz.) pkg. cream cheese, softened

1. Heat 3 tablespoons of the cream and liqueur in small saucepan over low heat until just simmering. Remove from heat; stir in chocolate chips. Continue stirring until smooth. Let cool.

2. In medium bowl, beat cream cheese and remaining 2 tablespoons cream at high speed until fluffy; beat in chocolate mixture. Divide between 2 (5-oz.) clear plastic beverage cups. Freeze several hours or overnight. Thaw before serving. Refrigerate leftovers.

2 servings

Pesto and Green Bean Potato Salad

Chocolate-Almond Mousse

Summery SALADS

by Carole Brown

Warm weather inspires each one of these salad ideas. But really, they'll go over successfully any time of year.

Lemon-Seafood Salad

selections

Lemon-Seafood Salad

**White Bean Salad
with Watercress**

**Herb and Mixed
Green Salad
with Fresh
Tomato Vinaigrette**

**Roast Asparagus
and Pasta Salad
with Parmesan Curls**

**Mango and
Grapefruit Salad**

Here are five ideas for
making salad something special ...
from something green to something fruity,
a selection with seafood, and more.

Lemon-Seafood Salad

The bright lemon, garlic and mustard flavors in this salad will make your guests sit up and take notice. This recipe makes a generous amount of lemon dressing, so you'll want to serve lots of good bread to soak up the extra.

COURT BOUILLON*
- 4 cups water
- 1 cup white wine or ½ cup white wine vinegar
- 1 small onion, sliced
- 1 rib celery, cut into chunks
- 2 garlic cloves, sliced
- 2 sprigs fresh thyme or 1 teaspoon dried
   Parsley stems
- 1 bay leaf
- 1 teaspoon salt
   Shrimp shells, if available

LEMON DRESSING
- 2 teaspoons finely chopped lemon peel
- ½ cup fresh lemon juice
- 1 teaspoon minced garlic
- 1 teaspoon salt
- 1 teaspoon ground white pepper
- 1 rounded tablespoon Dijon mustard
- 1 cup extra-virgin olive oil
   Dash hot pepper sauce

SALAD
- 2½ lb. shelled, deveined uncooked medium shrimp or sea scallops
- 2 cups rinsed trimmed Chinese pea pods
- 1 large red onion, very thinly sliced
- 1 cup ripe kalamata olives
- ⅓ cup chopped fresh parsley
- 1 (16-oz.) can grape or cherry tomatoes, rinsed, dried

> **TIP:**
>
> *Court bouillon ("short broth" in French) is a quick-cooking broth used to poach fish or vegetables. It is usually discarded after use. The onion, celery and garlic will add flavor, but they are not essential. Simply omit them if you don't have them on hand.

1. In large pot, combine water, wine, onion, celery, garlic, thyme, parsley, bay leaf, salt and shrimp shells. Simmer 20 to 30 minutes; strain. Discard bay leaf. Refrigerate bouillon for later use. Prepare lemon dressing while court bouillon is simmering.

2. To prepare dressing, combine lemon peel, lemon juice, garlic, salt, pepper and mustard. Whisk in olive oil and season with hot pepper sauce. Set aside.

3. Steam pea pods 2 to 3 minutes or until vibrant green. Refresh under cold water. Leave whole or cut into diagonal slices.

4. Bring bouillon to a gentle simmer in clean, large pot. Poach shrimp 3 to 6 minutes or just until shrimp curl and turn pink. Remove shrimp from bouillon; cool slightly. Discard bouillon.

5. In large bowl, combine shrimp, pea pods, sliced onion, olives and parsley. Add lemon dressing; toss gently. Refrigerate several hours. Garnish with tomatoes before serving.

8 servings

White Bean Salad with Watercress

Herb and Mixed Green Salad
with Fresh Tomato Vinaigrette

White Bean Salad with Watercress

This salad has a slightly French air about it, but it would be happy to share a plate with grilled Italian or Polish sausages or even American bratwursts. The peppery bite of watercress is ideal with the white beans, but you can substitute spinach if you have trouble finding watercress. The salad improves if you let it sit several hours or overnight before serving.

BEANS
- 1 lb. white beans, soaked overnight, drained
- 6 to 8 cups water
- 1½ teaspoons salt
- 1 bay leaf
- ½ teaspoon dried thyme

DRESSING
- ¼ cup fresh lemon juice
- 2 garlic cloves, minced
- 1 tablespoon Dijon mustard
- ¾ teaspoon salt
- ¼ teaspoon freshly ground pepper
- ½ cup olive oil or peanut oil
- ½ cup plain yogurt
- ½ large white or red onion, very thinly sliced
- 1 cup tightly packed coarsely chopped watercress

1. In large pot cover beans with water. Stir in salt, bay leaf and thyme. Bring to a simmer and cook, stirring occasionally, about 30 minutes or until beans are tender. Drain excess cooking liquid. Discard bay leaf.

2. Meanwhile, prepare dressing. In medium bowl, mix together lemon juice, yogurt, garlic, mustard, salt and pepper. Slowly whisk in oil.

3. In large bowl, combine warm beans with onion and watercress; toss gently. Stir in dressing; set aside to cool.

8 servings

Note:

If your beans are fresh you probably don't have to soak them before cooking. They may take slightly longer to cook, but that may be more convenient than soaking. Rinse beans in a colander under running water or swirl in a bowl of water to wash. Salt your water so the beans absorb more flavor as they cook. (Salt in the cooking water does not prevent the beans from softening.) For added color and flavor, add ½ cup diced red bell pepper or 1 cup diced ham.

Herb and Mixed Green Salad with Fresh Tomato Vinaigrette

Choose a bouquet of your favorite fresh herbs for this salad. To ensure that your salad won't wilt on a buffet table, dress only half of the salad. When that portion is gone, dress and serve the second half.

VINAIGRETTE
- 1 small shallot, sliced or 2 tablespoons chopped onion
- 1 tomato, seeded, coarsely chopped
- ¼ teaspoon salt
- ⅛ teaspoon freshly ground pepper
- 3 tablespoons wine vinegar
- ½ cup plus 1 tablespoon olive oil

SALAD
- 1 lb. baby mesclun or 2 large heads romaine or leaf lettuce, torn
- 2 to 3 cups mixed fresh herb leaves*
- ⅛ teaspoon salt
- ⅛ teaspoon freshly ground pepper

1. In blender, combine shallot, tomato, salt, pepper, vinegar and oil; process until smooth and color is bright orange.

2. Pour dressing into large bowl. Place salad greens and herbs on top of dressing; toss well, adding more dressing if desired. Season with salt and pepper. Toss again and serve.

8 to 10 servings

TIP:

*Some good fresh herb choices are: flat-leaf parsley, basil, chives, mint, oregano, marjoram, tarragon and watercress. Instead of mincing the herb leaves into little green pieces, leave them whole and mix them with salad greens. Your salad will come alive with all the fresh flavors of the season.

Roast Asparagus and Pasta Salad
with Parmesan Curls

Make this salad on the day you serve it, but the various elements can be prepared several hours ahead of time.

Notes:

Choose a medium-size dried pasta easy to eat in a salad; penne, ziti, farfalle and orecchiette would all be good choices. Roasted asparagus is superb in this salad, but you can use steamed or boiled asparagus if you prefer.

The Parmesan cheese is not just an afterthought here. Buy a block of the best cheese you can afford and shave off nice big curls. And just in case you are tempted to skip the bread crumbs, don't—their crunchy, nutty flavor tops the salad with real flair.

VINAIGRETTE
- 2   tablespoons finely minced shallots
       or ¼ cup minced onion
- 1   small garlic clove, minced
- 2   tablespoons water
- 2   tablespoons wine vinegar
- 2   teaspoons Dijon mustard
- ¼   teaspoon salt
       Dash cayenne pepper
- ⅛   teaspoon freshly ground pepper
- 2   tablespoons walnut oil
- ¼   cup canola oil

BREAD CRUMBS
- 1   cup dry plain or dry seasoned
       bread crumbs
- 3   tablespoons walnut oil

ASPARAGUS
- 1½ lb. asparagus, trimmed
- 1   to 2 tablespoons canola
       or vegetable oil
- ⅛   teaspoon salt
- ⅛   teaspoon freshly ground pepper

SALAD
- 8   oz. penne
- ⅛   teaspoon salt
- ⅛   teaspoon freshly ground pepper
- 1   cup (4 oz.) freshly grated
       Parmesan cheese
- 8   to 10 lettuce leaves

1. In small pot, heat shallots, garlic and water to a simmer over medium heat; cook until water evaporates. Stir in vinegar. Pour mixture into medium bowl. Stir in mustard, salt and hot pepper sauce; season with pepper. Whisk in oils. Set aside.

2. Moisten bread crumbs with 3 tablespoons of the oil, adding more if necessary, but avoid making crumbs heavy and oily. In large skillet over medium heat, toast crumbs, stirring occasionally. When crumbs start to brown, reduce heat to low. Stir and cook 5 to 8 minutes or until crumbs are crisp and golden brown. Pour out onto baking sheet or plate to cool. Set aside.

3. Rinse spears and pat dry. Depending on thickness of spears, choose one of the following methods for roasting: For thin asparagus spears, heat oven to 400°F. Place spears on baking sheet and drizzle with oil; roll spears in oil to cover evenly. Roast on rack in middle of oven 5 minutes; turn spears and roast an additional 2 to 3 minutes or until tender. Season with salt and pepper. For thick asparagus spears, heat broiler. Place spears on baking sheet and drizzle with oil; roll spears in oil to cover evenly. Broil 3 inches from heat 3 minutes. Turn spears; broil an additional 3 minutes or until tender. Season with salt and pepper.

4. When asparagus spears are cool enough to handle, cut into 1- or 2-inch lengths about the same size as pasta. Set aside. In large bowl, toss pasta with 5 to 6 tablespoons of the vinaigrette. Season with salt and pepper; set aside. With vegetable peeler or cheese slicer, shave large pieces or curls from Parmesan cheese. Set aside.

5. In another large bowl, gently toss pasta and asparagus. Add additional vinaigrette, if desired. Arrange lettuce leaves around sides of serving bowl. Sprinkle bread crumbs over salad. Top with shaved cheese.

8 (½ cup) servings

Mango and Grapefruit Salad

The sweet-and-sour flavors of mangoes and grapefruits make an irresistible salad, especially with a savory touch of herbs in the dressing. This salad is a wonderful choice any time of the year.

SALAD
- 2 large ripe mangoes
- 2 large red grapefruit

DRESSING
- ½ cup fresh orange/fresh grapefruit juice
- ¼ cup fresh lime juice
- ¼ cup honey
- Dash salt
- ½ teaspoon ground dried ginger
- 1 generous tablespoon chopped fresh herbs (chives, cilantro or parsley)
- ½ cup fresh grapefruit juice

1. Plane off bottoms of each mango to stabilize. Using knife or vegetable peeler, peel around mango from top down. Trim away bits of peel remaining on flesh. Stand mango on flat base; cut off two flat sides from large pit. Cut each mango half into diagonal slices, about ¼-inch wide.

2. Cut top and bottom off each grapefruit. Following contour of grapefruit, cut away peel and outer membrane in several downward slices around fruit. Trim away any small pieces of white membrane. Cut grapefruit segments out of surrounding membranes. When all segments have been removed, squeeze membrane over bowl to capture juice. Reserve grapefruit juice for dressing.

3. Spread fruit over platter, alternating mango and grapefruit slices. If any grapefruit segments are especially thick, slice in half lengthwise. Cover fruit with plastic wrap; store in refrigerator.

4. To prepare dressing, add orange and lime juices to grapefruit juice. Whisk in honey. Season with salt, ginger and herbs. Just before serving, pour dressing over fruit. Garnish platter with whole sprigs of herbs.

8 servings

Steak dinner

by Charla Draper

Why make things complicated?
Here's a complete steak dinner
that will please any group, any time.

menu

Seasoned Vegetable Grill

New Potato Salad with Blue Cheese Vinaigrette

Sizzlin' Southwestern Steak

Sensational Caramel Apple Crostata

Seasoned Vegetable Grill

Fresh grilled vegetables and an exciting potato salad make this menu much lighter than a traditional steak-and-taters feed. The Caramel Apple Crostata is, well, Sensational.

Seasoned Vegetable Grill

Summer vegetables, seasoned to skewer and grill, make for easy cooking and quick clean-up ... no dirty utensils, just toss away the skewers.

½ teaspoon seasoned salt
1 teaspoon ground cumin
½ teaspoon onion powder
¼ teaspoon freshly ground pepper
2 medium zucchini,
    cut into 1-inch pieces

2 medium summer squash,
    cut into 1-inch pieces
2 tablespoons melted butter
1 tablespoon chopped fresh cilantro
2 teaspoons fresh lime juice

Note:

To cook indoors, place meat on rack of broiler pan. Broil 6 to 8 minutes per side, 3 to 6 inches from heat.

1. Heat grill.

2. In small bowl, combine seasoned salt, cumin, onion powder and pepper. Pour over zucchini and squash in large bowl; toss well. Set aside 15 to 20 minutes.

3. In medium bowl, combine butter, cilantro and lime juice. Pour over seasoned vegetable mixture; toss well. Thread vegetables on skewers.

4. Place skewers on gas grill over medium heat or on charcoal grill 4 to 6 inches from coals. Grill 10 to 12 minutes or to desired doneness, turning once.

4 servings

New Potato Salad with Blue Cheese Vinaigrette

New potatoes and blue cheese turn the traditional steak and potatoes menu into contemporary fare. Potatoes and vegetables tossed with savory vinaigrette lighten up potato salad for the spring season.

SALAD
2 lb. new potatoes, cut into wedges
⅛ teaspoon salt
1 cup sliced celery
¼ cup chopped red onion
2 tablespoons chopped fresh parsley
2 tablespoons crumbled blue cheese

VINAIGRETTE
¼ cup white vinegar
½ teaspoon salt
¼ teaspoon sugar
¼ teaspoon minced garlic
⅛ teaspoon freshly ground pepper
⅛ teaspoon dry mustard
½ cup vegetable oil
2 tablespoons crumbled blue cheese

1. In large pot, cover potatoes with lightly salted water; bring to a boil over medium-high heat. Cook potatoes about 15 to 20 minutes or until fork-tender, drain. Set aside.

2. To prepare Vinaigrette, combine vinegar, salt, sugar, garlic, pepper and dry mustard in blender; process to blend. Turn blender setting to mix; slowly add oil. Scrape sides of blender jar, if necessary. Add 2 tablespoons blue cheese; process to blend.

3. Combine potatoes, celery, onion and parsley. Add vinegar mixture; stir gently. Chill several hours or overnight. Before serving, add remaining cheese; toss lightly. Garnish with red onion rings and additional fresh parsley.

6 servings

Sizzlin' Southwestern Steak

This dry rub offers flavors of the Southwest, updating sirloin steak with flair.

2 tablespoons chili powder	1 teaspoon salt
1 tablespoon crushed oregano	½ teaspoon onion powder
2 teaspoons ground cumin	1 (2-lb.) sirloin steak
1 teaspoon garlic powder	

Note:

Dry rubs are mixtures of spices spread on the surface of meat before cooking.

1. Heat grill.

2. In small bowl, combine chili powder, oregano, cumin, garlic powder, salt and onion powder; mix well. Spread seasoning mixture evenly over steak.

3. Place steak on gas grill over medium heat or on charcoal grill 4 to 6 inches from medium coals. Grill 8 to 10 minutes on each side or to desired doneness, turning once or heat broiler. Broil 3 to 6 inches from heat 8 to 10 minutes on each side, or to desired doneness.

4 to 6 servings

Sensational Caramel Apple Crostata

In this free form pastry, caramel and apples marry other All-American favorites for a delicious and easy dessert.

CRUST
2 cups all-purpose flour
3 tablespoons sugar
1 teaspoon salt
¾ cup shortening
⅓ cup cold milk
1 egg, separated
1 teaspoon fresh lemon juice

FILLING
½ cup sugar
½ cup packed brown sugar
¼ cup all-purpose flour
1 teaspoon cinnamon
1 teaspoon nutmeg
⅛ teaspoon salt
2 tablespoons butter
3½ cups peeled sliced apples
1 tablespoon fresh lemon juice
1 egg white
½ cup caramel topping

1. In large bowl, combine flour, 3 tablespoons sugar and 1 teaspoon salt; mix to blend. With pastry blender or two knives, cut in shortening until mixture crumbles.

2. In small bowl, combine milk, egg yolk and lemon juice. Add to flour mixture, gently stirring until flour mixture is moistened. Shape into ball; refrigerate 20 to 30 minutes or until firm.

3. Heat oven to 450°F.

4. Flatten dough ball to ½-inch thickness, rounding and smoothing edges. On lightly floured surface, with floured rolling pin, roll dough from center to edge forming 12- to 14-inch circle. Fold pastry in half; gently place on 15x10x1-inch baking sheet. Unfold and let edges of circles overlap pan edges. Set aside.

5. In medium bowl, combine ½ cup sugar, brown sugar, ¼ cup flour, cinnamon, nutmeg and ⅛ teaspoon salt. Cut in butter. Place apples in large bowl; sprinkle with lemon juice. Add sugar mixture to apples; mix.

6. Spoon apple mixture onto center of pastry, leaving 2-inch border. Fold edge of crust 2 inches over apples; crimp slightly. Brush crust with egg white. Sprinkle with 1 tablespoon sugar, if desired. Bake 20 to 25 minutes or until apples are tender and crust is golden brown. Cool completely on baking sheet. To serve, cut into wedges and spoon 1 tablespoon caramel topping onto each wedge.

6 to 8 servings

Sizzlin' Southwestern Steak

Sensational Caramel Apple Crostata

Marinades & More

by Lisa Golden Schroeder

Old standbys are fine, but when you're ready to get a little adventuresome in preparing meat for grilling, turn to these ideas.

Indonesian Marinade with Coconut-Peanut Finishing Sauce

selections

Blackberry Mustard Marinade

Indonesian Marinade with Coconut-Peanut Finishing Sauce

Cranberry-Maple Flavor Brine

Roasted Garlic-Herbed Paste

Apricot-Ginger Glaze with Balsamic Vinegar

Cinnamon-Chili Dry Rub

Usually all you need to make meat great is a little assistance here or there. These marinades—plus a brine, paste, glaze and rub—stand ready to help.

Blackberry Mustard Marinade

Summertime berries are fabulous in marinades for richer, sweeter meats like lamb or pork. To balance the sweetness, mustard and berry vinegar add tart components that complement the meat. Try lamb or pork loin chops, or pork tenderloin, in this jewel-toned marinade. Venison would also be great.

1	cup port wine	½	teaspoon salt
¼	cup Dijon mustard	¼	teaspoon freshly ground pepper
2	tablespoons raspberry or red wine vinegar	1½	lb. lamb, pork chops or pork tenderloin
2	tablespoons honey	1½	teaspoons cornstarch
2	tablespoons hazelnut, walnut or olive oil	2	cups fresh blackberries*
2	teaspoons minced fresh rosemary or mint		

TIP:

*Fresh ripe raspberries can replace the blackberries.

1. In large bowl, combine port, mustard, vinegar, honey, oil, rosemary, salt and pepper; mix well.

2. Pour marinade into large resealable plastic bag; add meat. Seal bag; refrigerate at least 2 hours or overnight, turning bag occasionally.

3. When ready to grill, remove meat from marinade. Pour marinade into medium saucepan; whisk in cornstarch. Bring mixture to a boil; cook and stir until sauce thickens. Stir in berries. Serve sauce with grilled meat.

2 cups

Indonesian Marinade with Coconut-Peanut Finishing Sauce

Marinate chicken breasts or try the suggestions below in this Asian-style marinade. After grilling, serve up the spicy Coconut-Peanut Finishing Sauce, rich with coconut milk and garlic, for dipping.

MARINADE

- ⅓ cup low-sodium soy sauce
- 2 tablespoons fresh lime juice
- 2 tablespoons honey
- 2 tablespoons chopped fresh cilantro
- 1 tablespoon grated fresh ginger
- 1 tablespoon sesame oil
- 1 lb. turkey tenderloins, duck breasts, small game hen halves or chicken wings

COCONUT-PEANUT FINISHING SAUCE

- 1 teaspoon honey
- 2 tablespoons water
- ⅓ cup peanut butter
- ½ cup coconut milk
- 2 tablespoons fresh lime juice
- ½ teaspoon minced garlic
- ½ teaspoon ground cumin
- ½ teaspoon hot pepper sauce

1. Combine soy sauce, lime juice, honey, cilantro, ginger, oil and turkey in large resealable plastic bag. Seal bag; refrigerate at least 2 hours, turning bag occasionally. Remove poultry from marinade. Discard remaining marinade.

2. To prepare sauce, combine honey, water, peanut butter, coconut milk, lime juice, garlic, cumin and hot pepper sauce in medium bowl; mix well. Serve with grilled turkey.

1¼ cups

Cranberry-Maple Flavor Brine

This technique of "flavor brining" differs from traditional brining that is done to preserve meat. By marinating the meat in the flavored brine (which is distinguished from a marinade by its higher salt and sugar concentration) for several hours, the meat's juiciness is increased along with the flavorings, which are carried into the meat with the salt water. Follow timing carefully for smaller cuts of meat, so they don't absorb too much of the salty flavor. Serve grilled meat with a cranberry relish, or applesauce with maple syrup.

Meat can be brined up to two days before grilling. Brine according to recipe, removing meat from brine when ready. Pat dry with paper towels; wrap in plastic wrap and refrigerate until ready to grill.

7	cups water	1	teaspoon vanilla
2	cups fresh cranberry juice	4	(1- to 1¼-lb.) pork tenderloins,
¾	cup pure maple syrup		1 (4- to 6-lb.) boneless pork loin
½	cup kosher (coarse) salt		roast or 6 (1¼- to 1½-inch-thick)
2	tablespoons freshly ground pepper		center-cut loin pork chops

1. In Dutch oven, heat water, juice, syrup and salt over medium heat until salt is dissolved. Remove from heat; stir in pepper and vanilla. Cover and cool brine in refrigerator.

2. Trim any excess fat from meat. Submerge meat in brine, making sure it stays below the surface, weighting it down with heavy plate, if needed. Refrigerate tenderloins 6 hours, roast 1 to 2 days or chops 4 to 6 hours.

3. Discard remaining brine; pat dry with paper towels. Allow meat to stand 30 minutes before grilling.

10 cups

Roasted Garlic-Herbed Paste

A thick paste of roasted garlic, spices and seasonal herbs is fragrant and flavorful on just about any poultry or meat. Freshly grind your spices using a mortar and pestle, or a clean spice or coffee grinder. The paste can be made ahead and keeps well, refrigerated in an airtight container, for up to 1 week.

1	cup tightly packed parsley sprigs	2	teaspoons kosher (coarse) salt
½	cup fresh sage	1	teaspoon toasted cumin seeds
½	cup fresh rosemary	1	teaspoon ground fennel seed
2	tablespoons roasted garlic paste*	½	teaspoon freshly ground pepper

1. In food processor, coarsely chop parsley, sage and rosemary. Add garlic paste, salt, cumin, fennel and pepper; process until smooth.

2. Generously rub mixture on chicken breasts, pork tenderloin, lamb chops, steaks or other meat before grilling.

Makes about 1¼ cups (for 1½ lb. poultry or meat)

TIP:

*To roast garlic, heat oven to 375°F. Slice tops off 2 cloves of garlic. Place cloves on sheet of aluminum foil and drizzle with olive oil. Close foil over garlic. Bake 40 to 45 minutes; cool. Squeeze soft, roasted garlic out of papery skins. Garlic should be soft enough to mash to a paste.

Apricot-Ginger Glaze with Balsamic Vinegar

Apricot-Ginger Glaze with Balsamic Vinegar

This glaze also makes a wonderful sauce. Mix all the ingredients in a small saucepan, cook over medium heat until hot and melted, stir in 1 cup diced fresh mango, then serve with grilled meat.

1 cup apricot preserves
2 tablespoons grated fresh ginger

1 teaspoon minced garlic
1 tablespoon balsamic vinegar

1. In small bowl, mix together preserves, ginger, garlic and vinegar. Brush mixture onto grilled pork, game hens or lamb during last 5 minutes of cooking.

1¼ cups (for 1 lb. poultry, meat or fish)

Cinnamon-Chili Dry Rub

Rub this spicy-sweet blend on chicken breasts, turkey breast or whole turkey, game hens or chicken wings. Look for pure ground chili powder in Latin American groceries or markets that stock a wide variety of herbs and spices.

6 tablespoons pure ground New Mexican red chili powder
2 tablespoons finely grated orange peel
1 tablespoon cinnamon

2 teaspoons toasted ground cumin seed
2 teaspoons dried marjoram
2 teaspoons kosher (coarse) salt
½ teaspoon garlic powder

Note:

For even brighter flavor, grind your own spices. Toast cumin seed in a dry skillet. Grind cinnamon sticks and the toasted cumin in a spice blender or clean coffee grinder.

1. In large bowl, combine chili powder, orange peel, cinnamon, cumin seed, marjoram, salt and garlic powder; mix well. Store in airtight container in refrigerator until ready to use.

2. Rub mixture onto or under skin of poultry before grilling.

½ cup

Burgers
Out of the Ordinary

By Mary Evans

Here's how to add new life
to the concept of "burgers."
There are enough ideas here to keep
any burger connoisseur happy.

Wild Rice and Mushroom Burgers with Red Pepper Mayonnaise

selections

Wild Rice and Mushroom Burgers with Red Pepper Mayonnaise

Oregon Blue Cheese Burgers

Teriyaki Tuna Burgers with Chili Mayonnaise

Lamb Burgers with Apricot-Mint Chutney

Chinese Pork Burgers with Double Plum Sauce

Hamburgers aren't just for beef anymore ... these ideas with tuna, pork and lamb (plus one meatless burger recipe) prove that. Okay, we threw in a beef recipe too, but gave it a heck of a twist.

Wild Rice and Mushroom Burgers with Red Pepper Mayonnaise

Buy roasted red bell peppers in a jar and keep on hand to add flavor and color to dishes. If unavailable, see the recipes for Goat Cheese, Roasted Pepper and Pine Nut Pâté (page 29) to make your own.

RED PEPPER MAYONNAISE
⅓ cup mayonnaise
3 tablespoons chopped roasted red bell peppers

BURGERS
2¾ cups water
1 extra-large vegetable bouillon cube or equivalent amount bouillon for 2 cups water

1 cup uncooked wild rice
2 cups sliced mushrooms
¼ teaspoon salt
¾ cup Italian seasoned dry bread crumbs
1 egg
4 slices provolone cheese
4 sliced buns

1. Heat grill.

2. In medium bowl, combine mayonnaise and bell peppers; mix well. Refrigerate, covered, until ready to serve.

3. In medium saucepan, bring water and bouillon cube to a boil over medium heat; stir to dissolve. Rinse and drain wild rice with cold water. Add rice to saucepan; cover and reduce heat to low. Cook about 1 hour or until wild rice kernels are opened and most or all liquid is absorbed. Rice should be slightly overcooked. Remove from heat and let cool. Drain if necessary.

4. Place wild rice, mushrooms and salt in food processor; process until mixture is finely chopped. Add ½ cup of the bread crumbs; pulse briefly to combine. Add egg; pulse briefly to combine. Shape mixture into 4 (1-inch thick) patties. Sprinkle remaining ¼ cup bread crumbs on small shallow plate. Dip patties into crumbs, coating both sides.

5. Place patties on gas grill over medium heat or on charcoal grill 4 to 6 inches from medium coals. Grill patties, covered, 6 minutes on each side or until piping hot in center. Top each burger with slice of provolone during last minute of cooking. Serve topped with red pepper mayonnaise and sautéed onions, if desired, on sliced buns.

4 servings

Oregon Blue Cheese Burgers

Choose a creamy-style blue cheese for these yummy burgers. Placing the blue cheese inside helps keep the burger moist while cooking. Make sure to press edges together well to prevent cheese from sticking. Serve with lettuce and sliced tomatoes for an updated California-style burger.

Note:

When choosing ground beef, the best flavor comes from meat no more than 80 percent lean.

3	tablespoons blue cheese	¼	teaspoon salt
2	tablespoons cream cheese, softened	⅛	teaspoon freshly ground pepper
1	teaspoon brandy	4	thick slices cooked bacon, halved
1¼	lb. ground beef	2	tablespoons butter
¼	cup chopped shallots	4	sliced buns

1. Heat grill. Brush lightly with oil.

2. In small bowl, combine blue cheese, cream cheese and brandy until creamy. Set aside.

3. In medium bowl, mix together ground beef, shallots, salt and pepper. Divide into 8 sections. Shape each section into flat patty. Spoon blue cheese mixture evenly into centers of 4 patties. Cover with remaining patties, pressing to seal edges and shaping into 4 (¾-inch thick) patties.

4. Place patties on gas grill over medium heat or on charcoal grill 4 to 6 inches from medium coals. Grill patties, covered, 5 minutes on each side or until no longer pink in center. Top each with ½ strip bacon during last 2 minutes of cooking. Serve on lightly buttered sliced buns.

4 servings

Teriyaki Tuna Burgers with Chile Mayonnaise

Look for chili paste or chili sauce with garlic in the Asian section of your grocery store. Don't confuse it with the tomato-based, cocktail style chili sauce.

CHILI MAYONNAISE
½ cup mayonnaise
1½ to 2 teaspoons Asian chili paste or chili sauce with garlic

BURGERS
1¼ lb. tuna steaks, cut into 1-inch pieces
2 tablespoons low-sodium soy sauce
1 tablespoon vegetable oil
1 tablespoon dry sherry or white wine
2 teaspoons finely minced garlic
1 teaspoon finely minced ginger
4 sliced sesame buns

1. Heat grill.

2. Stir together mayonnaise and chili paste in small bowl. Refrigerate, covered, until ready to serve.

3. In food processor, process tuna until coarsely ground. Transfer tuna to medium bowl; stir in soy sauce, oil, sherry, garlic and ginger until just combined. Shape into 4 (1-inch thick) patties.

4. Place patties on gas grill over medium heat or on charcoal grill 4 to 6 inches from medium coals. Grill patties, covered, about 4 minutes on each side or until no longer pink in center. Serve topped with chili mayonnaise on sliced sesame buns.

4 servings

Teriyaki Tuna Burgers with Chili Mayonnaise

Lamb Burgers with Apricot-Mint Chutney

Chinese Pork Burgers with Double Plum Sauce

Lamb Burgers with Apricot-Mint Chutney

These burgers capture Moroccan flavors in your own backyard. Called *kefta* in Morocco, this mixture translates well to American grilling.

APRICOT-MINT CHUTNEY
1 (15-oz.) can chopped
    apricots, drained
2 tablespoons fresh lemon juice
2 tablespoons honey
2 tablespoons chopped mint

BURGERS
1¼ lb. ground lamb
¼ cup finely chopped green onion
2 tablespoons chopped
    fresh Italian parsley
2 tablespoons chopped fresh cilantro
1 teaspoon ground cumin
½ teaspoon salt
½ teaspoon allspice
¼ teaspoon cinnamon
⅛ teaspoon cayenne pepper

1. Heat grill.

2. In medium saucepan, combine apricots, lemon juice and honey; cook over medium heat about 4 minutes or until thickened. Remove from heat; stir in mint. Set aside.

3. In medium bowl, mix together lamb, green onion, parsley, cilantro, cumin, salt, allspice, cinnamon and cayenne pepper until well combined. Shape into 4 (1-inch thick) patties.

4. Place patties on gas grill over medium heat or on charcoal grill 4 to 6 inches from medium coals. Grill patties, covered, 5 minutes on each side or until no longer pink in center. Serve topped with Apricot-Mint Chutney on sliced onion buns.

4 servings

Chinese Pork Burgers with Double Plum Sauce

Hoisin sauce, plum sauce and five-spice powder are commonly used ingredients in Chinese cooking, and have become increasingly available. Look for five-spice powder in the spice section or Asian section of the grocery store.

BURGERS
1¼ lb. ground pork
¼ cup chopped green onions
2 tablespoons hoisin sauce
½ teaspoon five-spice powder
4 sliced buns

DOUBLE PLUM SAUCE
1 plum, pitted, cut into 4 lengthwise
    slices
¼ cup plum sauce

1. Heat grill.

2. In large bowl, mix together pork, green onions, hoisin sauce and five-spice powder until well combined. Shape into 4 (1-inch thick) patties.

3. Place patties on gas grill over medium heat or on charcoal grill 4 to 6 inches from medium coals. Grill patties, covered, about 5 minutes on each side or until no longer pink in center.

4. Meanwhile, add plum slices to grill; grill 5 minutes, turning once. Remove and chop into ¼-inch pieces. Combine with plum sauce in small bowl. Serve pork burgers topped with double plum sauce on sliced buns.

4 servings

Fourth of July Party

by Charla Draper

If your heart already beats true for the red, white and blue, then this menu will make your tastebuds pick up the pace too.

menu

Rosemary-Garlic Lamb

Crimson Pepper Dip and Pitas

Savory Polenta

Ratatouille Salad

Summer Fruit 'N Berry Crisp

Rosemary-Garlic Lamb

The colors in this menu add appetite appeal to Independence Day, but the tastes—from Rosemary-Garlic Grilled Lamb to Summer Fruit 'N Berry Crisp—are suitable at any celebration.

Rosemary-Garlic Lamb

Lamb continues to gain popularity on the American menu. For grilling a leg of lamb, "butterfly" the meat: Remove the bone and open the meat to a flatter portion. This will reduce your grilling time.

¾ **cup olive oil**	1 **teaspoon salt**
¼ **cup plus 2 tablespoons red wine**	½ **teaspoon grated lemon peel**
2 **tablespoons minced garlic**	¼ **teaspoon freshly ground pepper**
¼ **cup minced fresh rosemary**	1 **(4- to 6-lb.) leg of lamb, butterflied**
¼ **cup chopped shallots**	

1. In medium jar, combine oil, wine, garlic, rosemary, shallots, salt, lemon peel and pepper; cover and shake until well blended.

2. Place meat in large bowl or shallow dish; pour oil mixture over meat. Cover; marinate in refrigerator overnight, turning occasionally to coat meat.

3. Heat grill. Remove lamb from marinade; place meat on gas grill over medium heat or on charcoal grill 4 to 6 inches from medium coals. Sear meat on both sides 4 to 5 minutes or until browned. Continue cooking, turning occasionally, until internal temperature reaches 160°F. Remove from grill; let rest 15 to 20 minutes before carving.

6 to 8 servings

Crimson Pepper Dip and Pitas

Crimson Pepper Dip, with its color and zingy taste, sparks this 4th of July menu.

1 **red bell pepper, halved lengthwise**	½ **teaspoon salt**
1 **(8 oz.) pkg. cream cheese, softened**	¼ **teaspoon freshly ground pepper**
¼ **cup (1 oz.) feta cheese**	¼ **to ½ teaspoon hot pepper sauce**
2 **tablespoons green onion slices**	**Pita Bread, quartered**
1 **teaspoon celery seed**	**Olive oil**

1. Place pepper, cut side down on broiler pan, 6 inches from heat. Broil 6 to 8 minutes, until pepper chars. Remove from broiler. Using tongs, place hot pepper in resealable plastic bag; seal bag. Let cool 15 to 20 minutes. Remove pepper from bag; peel away charred skin. Cut peeled pepper into chunks.

2. In food processor, combine red pepper chunks, cream cheese, feta cheese, green onion slices, celery seed, salt, pepper and hot pepper sauce; process until well blended. Chill mixture several hours or overnight.

3. Heat grill. Brush bread lightly with oil on each side. Place on gas grill over medium heat or on charcoal grill 4 to 6 inches from medium coals until lightly browned. Serve pita wedges with Crimson Pepper Dip and vegetable dippers.

1⅓ cups

Savory Polenta

Polenta is a staple in Northern Italian cuisine. Basically a mush prepared from cornmeal, this version uses standard cornmeal. The traditional finely ground dry meal of Italy can be found in gourmet food stores or Italian markets.

1	(14½-oz.) can reduced-sodium vegetable or chicken broth	2	tablespoons freshly grated Parmesan cheese
1	cup water	⅛	teaspoon freshly ground pepper
¾	cup cornmeal	1	teaspoon vegetable oil
2	tablespoons chopped fresh parsley		

1. Spray 8-inch square pan with nonstick cooking spray.

2. In large saucepan, heat broth and water over medium heat until mixture boils. Gradually stir in cornmeal until mixture is smooth. Stir in parsley, cheese and pepper. Reduce heat to low; cover. Continue cooking 5 to 7 minutes or until thickened, stirring occasionally.

3. Remove from heat; pour cornmeal mixture into pan. Refrigerate overnight or until mixture is firm.

4. Heat grill. Cut polenta into 4 squares; cut each square diagonally into 2 triangles. Place on lightly greased gas grill over medium heat or on charcoal grill 4 to 6 inches from medium coals. Cook, turning once, 4 to 6 minutes or until lightly browned. Remove from grill; serve with Ratatouille Salad and Rosemary Garlic Lamb.

6 to 8 servings

Ratatouille Salad

Ratatouille (ra-ta-too-ye) Salad is a versatile menu addition that can be served hot or cold. Prepared from sun-kissed vegetables with fresh herbs and balsamic vinegar, making one day ahead eases your preparation time and maximizes flavor.

1	(1-lb.) eggplant	3	cups diced tomato
¼	cup balsamic vinegar	½	cup chopped green bell pepper
2	teaspoons minced garlic	2	tablespoons chopped fresh basil
½	teaspoon salt		

1. Heat grill. Peel and slice eggplant into ½-inch slices. Pour vinegar into large bowl. Dip each eggplant slice into vinegar, coating both sides. Reserve remaining vinegar; set aside.

2. Place eggplant slices on gas grill over medium heat or on charcoal grill 4 to 6 inches from medium coals. Cook, turning once, 8 to 10 minutes. Remove from grill; cool. Cube each slice.

3. Add garlic and salt to reserved vinegar. Add eggplant, tomatoes, bell pepper and basil, mixing lightly to blend. Chill several hours or overnight. Serve over Savory Polenta or lettuce with freshly grated Parmesan cheese, if desired.

6 servings

Ratatouille Salad

Summer Fruit 'N Berry Crisp

Summer Fruit 'N Berry Crisp

This summer fruit crisp adds patriotic red, white and blue to the 4th of July table.

2 **cups sliced fresh peaches**	¾ **cup all-purpose flour**
1 **cup fresh blueberries**	⅔ **cup sugar**
1 **cup fresh raspberries**	3 **tablespoons chopped almonds**
½ **cup sugar**	½ **teaspoon cinnamon**
2 **tablespoons tapioca**	½ **teaspoon salt**
1 **teaspoon fresh lemon juice**	1 **egg**
½ **teaspoon cinnamon**	1 **tablespoon milk**
½ **teaspoon grated lemon peel**	2 **tablespoons melted butter**
¼ **cup old-fashioned rolled oats**	

1. Heat oven to 400°F. In large bowl, combine fruit; set aside. In small bowl, combine sugar, tapioca, lemon juice and lemon peel; mix until blended. Pour mixture over fruit; stir gently. Spoon fruit into 2-quart casserole.

2. In medium bowl, combine flour, sugar, oats, 2 tablespoons of the almonds, cinnamon and salt, mix well. Stir in egg and milk; mix just until blended. Crumble over fruit mixture; sprinkle with remaining 1 tablespoon nuts. Drizzle with butter. Bake 20 to 30 minutes or until golden brown; cool completely on wire rack. Serve with whipped cream, if desired. Garnish with additional raspberries and blueberries.

4 to 6 servings

Summer Smoked Meats

by Beatrice Ojakangas

*You don't need to be a professional
to create great smoked meats.
All you need is a smoker
(not that expensive!)
and these ideas to get started.*

Smoked Beef Brisket

Summertime is a great time for smoking meats like salmon, turkey, beef and pork. And there are always plenty of occasions where you can feature your creations!

Smoked Beef Brisket

This recipe starts out from scratch with a fresh beef brisket. You can also use this smoke-cooking technique for store-purchased brined corned beef. Most commercially brined corned beef, however, is much saltier than this one.

1	(4- to 6-lb.) untrimmed beef brisket	2	bay leaves
1	cup red wine vinegar	2	ribs celery with leaves, chopped
1	cup water	2	crushed juniper berries
1	large onion, sliced	1	tablespoon mixed dried Italian-style
2	garlic cloves, minced		herbs (basil, rosemary and thyme)
8	whole cloves	1	tablespoon packed brown sugar
6	sprigs fresh parsley	1	tablespoon kosher (coarse) salt

1. Wash and dry meat. Place meat in large bowl. Combine vinegar, water, onion, garlic, cloves, parsley, bay leaves, celery, juniper berries, Italian herbs, brown sugar and salt; pour over meat. Refrigerate, covered, 24 to 48 hours. Remove from refrigerator 2 hours before smoke-cooking. Discard bay leaves.

2. Heat smoker according to manufacturer's instructions. If you are using charcoal smoker, this recipe will require a full pan of briquettes.

3. Soak wood chips, mesquite, hickory or fruitwood chips at least 1 hour. Add presoaked wood chips or chunks to heat source (charcoal, gas or electric). Fill pan to within ½ inch of top with hot water.

4. Place meat on highest cooking rack. Cover and smoke-cook at low heat (180°F to 200°F) 8 to 10 hours or until meat is fork-tender. Remove from smoker and serve warm or cooled, cut into thin, crosswise slices. Offer freshly grated horseradish with meat. Makes 4 servings per pound.

16 to 24 servings

Brown Sugar-Brined Smoked Turkey with Garlic-Raisin Sauce

Brining simply means that the turkey is soaked in a sugar-salt brine solution overnight. This step produces juicy, succulent meat. This turkey is delicious served with a simple-to-prepare garlic raisin sauce.

Note:

Use a smoker that has a thermometer on the lid and registers in degrees. Smokers are fueled with either charcoal, gas jets or with an electric burner, and have a water pan that sits above the heat source.

TURKEY
1 (12-lb.) fresh turkey
3 quarts water
2 cups packed brown sugar
½ cup salt
3 garlic cloves

GARLIC RAISIN SAUCE
1 (8-oz.) can tomato sauce
3 tablespoons packed brown sugar

6 garlic cloves, minced
⅛ to ½ teaspoon cayenne pepper
¼ cup cider vinegar
1¼ cups golden raisins
⅓ cup water

STUFFING
1 onion, peeled
4 sprigs fresh parsley
3 sprigs fresh rosemary

1. Rinse turkey and pat dry. Place in deep plastic, glass or stainless steel container large enough to immerse turkey in brining solution.

2. In large bowl, combine water, brown sugar, salt and garlic; stir until sugar and salt dissolve. Pour over turkey, covering completely. Cover with plastic wrap. Refrigerate overnight.

3. Meanwhile, in food processor, combine tomato sauce, brown sugar, garlic, cayenne pepper, vinegar, raisins and water; process until smooth. Pour into saucepan; bring to a boil. Cook, stirring, until reduced to 1½ cups; cool. Cover and refrigerate until cold.

4. Drain turkey and pat dry. Stuff cavity with onion, parsley and rosemary. Close opening; secure legs.

5. Heat smoker according to the manufacturer's instructions. If you are using a charcoal smoker, this recipe will require a full pan of briquets.

6. Soak wood chips, mesquite, hickory or fruitwood chips at least 1 hour. Add presoaked wood chips or chunks to heat source (charcoal, gas or electric). Fill pan to within ½ inch of the top with hot water.

7. Place turkey on highest cooking rack; cover and smoke 6 to 8 hours at low heat (200°F to 225°F) or until instant-read thermometer inserted into thickest part of thigh reads 180°F.

8. Remove turkey from grill to platter; remove and discard stuffing. Carve and serve with cold garlic raisin sauce.

1½ cups sauce

Brown Sugar-Brined Smoked Turkey with Garlic-Raisin Sauce

Honey Brined Alder-Smoked Salmon

Honey Brined Alder-Smoked Salmon

Alder wood is the classic smoker-wood for salmon, used by Native Americans for generations. As opposed to the other smoked items in this section, this salmon is smoked in slow, dry heat without a water pan.

1	quart water	10	whole cloves
½	cup salt	10	peppercorns
¾	cup honey	10	allspice berries
¼	cup golden or light rum	1	bay leaf
¼	cup fresh lemon juice	1	(1¾-lb.) salmon fillet

1. In large bowl, combine water, salt, honey, rum, lemon juice, cloves, peppercorns, berries and bay leaf. Add salmon, skin side up and refrigerate 2 hours. (If you marinate overnight, reduce salt to ¼ cup). Drain salmon and pat dry. Place on rack and allow to air-dry 1 hour.

2. Heat dry smoker. Add presoaked wood chips to heat source (or onto top of charcoal). Place salmon with skin side down on highest rack. Cover and smoker-cook about 1½ hours or until salmon is firm, maintaining temperature between 150°F and 170°F. Serve warm or well-chilled. Garnish with capers and lemon slices.

4 to 6 main dish servings   8 to 12 appetizer servings

Spiced Beer-Smoked Pork

As the pork smokes to tender succulence, beer in the water pan adds moisture and a rich, yeasty flavor and aroma. For the juiciest and tenderest of meat, select a pork roast that has a good covering of fat.

1	(6-lb.) boneless pork shoulder or loin of pork	1	teaspoon freshly ground pepper
2	tablespoons packed brown sugar	1	teaspoon ground allspice
1	tablespoon ground cumin	1	teaspoon crushed bay leaves
2	teaspoons kosher (coarse) salt	½	teaspoon dried marjoram
1	teaspoon ground cloves	¼	cup Worcestershire sauce
1	teaspoon dried oregano	⅔	cup red wine vinegar
		2	(12-oz.) cans beer

1. Place pork in large bowl. In medium bowl, combine sugar, cumin, salt, cloves, oregano, pepper, allspice, bay leaves and marjoram; mix well. Rub mixture thoroughly onto meat. Cover and refrigerate overnight. Two hours before smoking meat, remove from refrigerator and pour Worcestershire sauce and vinegar over pork; rub into pork well. Let stand at room temperature, turning frequently, while preparing smoker.

2. Heat smoker according to manufacturer's instructions. If using charcoal smoker, this recipe will require a full pan of briquets.

3. Soak wood chips, mesquite, hickory or fruitwood chips for at least 1 hour. Add presoaked wood chips or chunks to heat source (charcoal, gas or electric). Put water pan in place; add beer and enough water to fill pan.

4. Remove meat from marinade and place on highest food rack in smoker. Cover and smoker-cook 6 hours or until meat is fork-tender, maintaining temperature between 200°F and 225°F. Refill water pan. Add additional coals and wood chips to fire as needed. Cook an additional 2½ to 3 hours or until meat is fork-tender and no longer pink in center. To serve, cut across grain into thin slices.

8 to 10 servings

A *Southern* CELEBRATION

by Jim Casada

This down-home feast is traditionally served on the first day of dove hunting season, one of the most important social occasions of the year in the South. Everybody attends!

menu

Low Country Shrimp Boil

Country Cooked Green Beans with Ham Hock

Squash Fritters

Venison Meatballs in Currant Sauce

Dilly Potato Salad

Lemon Chess Pie

Low Country Shrimp Boil

Here are real flavors of the South, a homey and hearty culinary adventure you need to taste just once ... and then you'll have to do it again and again.

Low Country Shrimp Boil

Seafood looms large in Southern cooking, and this dish from the Carolina coast is hearty, easily prepared and ideally suited for consumption in an outdoor setting. It combines shrimp, smoked sausage, corn on the cob, potatoes, celery and onions with spices. Boiled together, the result is a union of flavors which will, as an old-timer once put it, "bring tears of pure joy to the eyes of a country boy."

3 lb. smoked sausage or kielbasa, cut into 1-inch pieces*	3 ribs celery, cut into 2-inch pieces
8 potatoes, cut into 2-inch pieces	4 tablespoons Old Bay seasoning
3 onions, cut into 2-inch pieces	10 to 12 ears corn, halved
	5 lb. shrimp**

1. Fill large pot half full of water; bring to a boil over medium-high heat. Cook sausage, potatoes, onions, celery and Old Bay seasoning 20 minutes or until potatoes are fork-tender. Add corn and shrimp; boil 3 to 4 minutes or until shrimp turn pink.

2. Drain and serve immediately on large platters from which guests can serve themselves. Melted butter and seafood sauce complement the meal.

10 to 12 servings

TIP:
*If you prefer, use smoked venison sausage.

TIP:
**In addition to shrimp, you can add crab legs or other shellfish.

Country Cooked Green Beans with Ham Hock

Green beans have always been a staple of Southern cuisine, and in days of yesteryear they were even dried and stored for winter to use as "leather britches," as this version was commonly called. For the true soul of the South though, one need look no further than a steaming pot of green beans that have simmered with a hefty ham hock to accompany them.

8 cups broken fresh green beans, rinsed	1 large ham hock*
	1 tablespoon salt

1. Place beans in large pot with enough water to cover. Add ham hock; bring to a boil over medium-high heat. Cover, reduce heat and simmer rapidly 1 hour. Check pot occasionally, adding water if beans start to boil dry. After an hour, add salt.

2. Remove ham hock from beans; cool slightly. Separate lean and fat meat in the hock by pulling with two forks. Add shredded lean meat back to green beans; stir well. Cover and simmer slowly an additional 1 hour.

6½ cups

TIP:
*Although not quite so tasty, bacon or fat back can be substituted for ham hock.

Squash Fritters

Squash Fritters

Southern cooks have long been known for their penchant for fried foods, and rightly so. Yet *fried* does not necessarily mean *swimming in grease*, and squash fritters are an excellent example. These fritters utilize one of the most easily grown and prolific of all vegetables in a taste-tempting fashion.

4 **cups grated yellow summer squash***	4 **tablespoons melted margarine**
½ **cup finely chopped onion**	1 **cup (4 oz.) grated cheddar cheese**
1 **teaspoon salt**	⅛ **teaspoon freshly ground pepper**
1 **cup all-purpose flour**	**Canola oil**
4 **eggs, beaten**	

1. In large bowl, combine squash, onion, salt and flour; mix well. Stir in eggs and margarine; mix well. Add cheese; continue stirring until ingredients are combined. Season with pepper.

2. In large skillet, heat enough oil to prevent sticking over medium-high heat until hot. Drop mixture by large tablespoonfuls, 5 fritters at once, into skillet; cook until squash is tender and fritters are golden brown on both sides. Serve hot.

24 (3x3-inch) fritters

TIP:

*This recipe works equally well for zucchini. The only real difference is that your fritters will be green instead of yellow.

Venison Meatballs in Currant Sauce

This tasty hors d'oeuvre offers an ideal way to clean out any ground venison still remaining in your freezer from the previous fall of hunting or, should you be among those unfortunate souls lacking deer meat, ground beef can be substituted. If the suggested portions seem large, there's a reason. Hunters have hefty appetites, and rest assured any remaining meatballs will magically vanish after your event's conclusion.

MEATBALLS
1½ **lb. ground venison**
½ **cup dry bread crumbs**
½ **cup milk**
1 **egg, beaten**
¼ **cup finely minced onion**
1½ **teaspoons salt**

¼ **teaspoon freshly ground pepper**
1 **teaspoon minced garlic**

SAUCE*
1 **(10-oz.) jar red currant jelly**
1 **(12-oz.) jar chili sauce**

1. Heat oven to 350°F.

2. In large bowl, combine venison, bread crumbs, milk, egg, onion, salt, pepper and garlic; mix well. Shape into 1-inch meatballs. Place meatballs into 13x9-inch casserole; bake 30 minutes or until no longer pink in center. Drain well, if needed.

3. In large skillet, combine jelly and chili sauce; add meatballs and simmer 30 minutes. Serve hot in chafing dish.

40 to 50 meatballs

TIP:

*If you prefer, you can use a slow cooker for the sauce. Heat sauce and jelly until the jelly melts; add chili sauce and cooked meatballs, then cook on low heat setting for 4 to 6 hours. Prepared this way, the meatballs really absorb the flavor of the sauce. Meatballs can be made in advance, cooked and frozen. Thaw completely before adding to sauce, to prevent meatballs from breaking apart.

Dilly Potato Salad

Although the Low Country Shrimp Boil includes potatoes, no outdoor meal in the Southern heartland would be complete without some sort of potato salad. Potatoes are a standby in most gardens, and folks long accustomed to putting up pickles usually grow dill as well. Easily prepared in advance, this dish uses the distinctive taste of fresh dill to add a special flavor and flair. The result is a novel way to offer an old favorite.

TIP:

* If you do not like raw onions, cook the minced onion with the potatoes.

½ cup mayonnaise	½ teaspoon freshly ground pepper
½ cup sour cream	4 to 5 cups cooked sliced potatoes
3 tablespoons cider vinegar	½ cup finely minced onion*
2 tablespoons sugar	4 to 6 hard-cooked eggs, sliced
1 tablespoon chopped fresh dill	
1 teaspoon salt	

1. In large bowl, combine mayonnaise, sour cream, vinegar, sugar, dill, salt and pepper; mix well. Add cooked potatoes, onions and eggs; toss gently to coat. Cover and chill. Garnish with additional dill, if desired.

6 cups

Lemon Chess Pie

Cooks in the region below the Mason-Dixon line have long catered to the dictates of menfolks' "sweet tooth" with simple-yet-scrumptious pies using readily available ingredients. Berry pies and cobblers come immediately to mind, as do egg-rich renditions, such as buttermilk pie or brown sugar pie. This savory recipe provides a perfect end to a dove shoot feast, or any other culinary get-together.

2 cups sugar	¼ cup milk
¼ cup butter, melted	½ cup fresh lemon juice
1 tablespoon all-purpose flour	1 tablespoon grated lemon peel
1 tablespoon cornmeal	1 (9-inch) frozen pie shell
4 eggs	

1. Heat oven 350°F. Spray 9-inch pie plate with nonstick cooking spray.

2. In large bowl, combine sugar, butter, flour and cornmeal; mix until well blended. Add eggs, one at a time, beating well at medium speed. Add milk, lemon juice and lemon peel; stir well. Pour mixture into pie shell. Bake 40 minutes to 1 hour or until firm in center.

6 to 8 servings

Lemon Chess Pie

Fish on the GRILL

by Lisa Golden Schroeder

Here's how to cook fresh summertime fish outside, on the grill, out of the hot kitchen. Find a great fish feature recipe right here.

Moroccan Cured Salmon

Fish

Moroccan
Cured Salmon

Swordfish with
Artichoke Tapenade

Halibut with
Hoisin-Sesame
Glaze

Grilled
Basque Fish
Packets

Grilling fish can dry out the meat
and render it tasteless. But these
recipes avoid all that by adding
moisture and paying careful attention
to how long you cook the fish.

Moroccan Cured Salmon

The technique of curing uses salt as a medium to draw some of the moisture out of the fish, while Moroccan-style spices add exotic flavor. If the cure is left on long enough, the fish will actually "cook," like gravlax or ceviche. Here the salmon retains enough moisture so it isn't dry, and the sugar from the cure gives the fish a delicious crispness.

CURE MIX
- ½ lb. kosher (coarse) salt
- 1 (16-oz.) pkg. packed brown sugar
- 2 tablespoons garlic powder
- 2 tablespoons onion powder
- 2 tablespoons ground ginger
- 2 tablespoons ground cumin
- 2 tablespoons ground coriander
- 1 tablespoon ground cloves
- 1 teaspoon ground turmeric

SALMON
- 4 (6-oz.) salmon fillets
- 2 tablespoons vegetable oil

1. Heat grill.

2. In blender, combine salt, brown sugar, garlic powder, onion powder, ginger, cumin, coriander, cloves and turmeric; mix thoroughly until smooth. Store in airtight container until ready to use. (You can store any unused cure mix up to 1 year.)

3. Rub fillets with enough of the mixture to cover thoroughly. Cure salmon 2 to 4 hours in covered container in refrigerator. (Cure for longer amount of time for thicker fillets and stronger flavor. For moist but milder-flavored fish, cure a shorter time.) To stop curing process, rinse salmon with cold water and brush with vegetable oil.

4. Place fish on gas grill over medium heat or on charcoal grill 4 to 6 inches from hot coals. Grill fish fillets 7 to 10 minutes or until fish flakes easily with fork.

4 (6-oz.) fillets

Swordfish with Artichoke Tapenade

The unmistakable flavors of the Mediterranean meet in this sauce. More pungent niçoise, kalamata, or other Greek or Spanish olives could replace the milder ripe olives.

- 2 tablespoons olive oil
- 2 teaspoons fresh lemon juice
- 4 (6-oz.) swordfish steaks
- ⅛ teaspoon freshly ground pepper
- 1 (6.5-oz.) jar marinated artichoke hearts
- ¼ cup pitted ripe olives
- ¼ cup oil-packed, sun-dried tomatoes, drained
- ½ cup chopped fresh parsley
- 1 teaspoon grated lemon peel

1. Heat grill.

2. In small bowl, combine olive oil and lemon juice. Brush mixture on both sides of each fish steak. Season with pepper.

3. Place fish on gas grill over medium-high heat or on charcoal grill 4 to 6 inches from medium coals. Cook 8 to 10 minutes, turning once, or until fish flakes easily with fork.

4. Meanwhile, in food processor, combine artichoke hearts with marinade, olives, sun-dried tomatoes, parsley and lemon peel; process until nearly smooth. Serve over hot grilled fish.

4 (6-oz.) steaks

Note:
If you can't find swordfish, any other firm-fleshed fish would be great: mahi-mahi, shark, halibut or sea bass.

Halibut with Hoisin-Sesame Glaze

Hoisin sauce, rice wine vinegar and sesame oil can all be found in the Asian section of most supermarkets. Hoisin is a dark, thick, sweet paste made from soybeans, sugar, spices and chiles. Its denseness melts into a glaze that creates a caramelized coating on the fish as it grills. Serve the fish with hot cooked soba (buckwheat) or whole wheat noodles, grilled green onions and mushrooms, and steamed spinach.

TIP:

*Look for black (unhulled) sesame seeds in Asian markets or co-ops.

½   cup hoisin sauce
2   tablespoons freshly grated ginger
2   tablespoons rice wine vinegar
1   tablespoon sesame oil
½   teaspoon ground coriander

4   (6- to 8-oz.) halibut steaks, sea bass fillets or tuna steaks
2   tablespoons toasted white and/or black sesame seeds*

1. Heat grill.

2. In small bowl, combine hoisin, ginger, vinegar, oil and coriander; mix well.

3. Place fish on gas grill over medium heat or on charcoal grill 4 to 6 inches from medium coals. Brush sauce on fish; cover and cook 5 minutes. Turn fish, brush with sauce and cover again. Cook an additional 5 minutes or until fish flakes easily with fork.

4. Serve fish hot, sprinkled with sesame seeds and chopped fresh cilantro.

4 steaks   scant ¾ cup sauce

Grilled Basque Fish Packets

These individual packets of tender white fish are great for entertaining. The flavors of Spain—a bit of spicy green chile, tomato, orange and olives—will stir up appetites. Serve alongside hot, fluffy rice tossed with toasted almonds and fennel seed, and sprinkled with crumbled feta cheese.

1   tablespoon olive oil
1   large red onion, halved, thinly sliced
3   garlic cloves, minced
1   (14.5-oz.) can diced tomatoes
2   oranges
¼   cup diced green chiles

12 large pimiento-stuffed olives, halved
½   teaspoon salt
¼   teaspoon freshly ground pepper
6   large red potatoes, thinly sliced
1   lb. red snapper fillet, cut into 4 pieces

Note:

Cod, orange roughy, trout or catfish fillets could be substituted for the red snapper.

1. Heat grill.

2. In large skillet, heat oil over medium-high heat until hot; sauté onion and garlic 4 minutes or until nearly tender. Stir in tomatoes with juice. Reduce heat to low; simmer 6 to 8 minutes.

3. Grate peel from oranges. Peel away remaining skin and cut oranges into segments, catching any juices in small bowl. Stir orange peel, orange segments, orange juice, chiles and olives into tomato sauce. Season with salt and pepper; cool mixture slightly.

4. Meanwhile, tear off 8 (12-inch) pieces of heavy-duty aluminum foil. Arrange ¼ of the potato slices in an even layer on 4 pieces of foil. Place one piece of fish on each piece of foil. Top each with ¼ of the sauce. Cover each with another piece of foil; seal edges tightly.

5. Place packets on baking sheet to transfer to and from grill. Place foil packets on gas grill over medium heat or on charcoal grill 4 to 6 inches from medium coals. Cover grill; cook 15 to 20 minutes, rearranging packets on grill halfway through cooking time, or until fish flakes easily with fork.

Halibut with Hoisin-Sesame Glaze

Ice Cream Social

by Carole Brown

Forget about all the other goodies, we only want ice cream! So that's all you'll find in the recipe repertoire that follows—great ideas for cold summer treats.

selections

**Blueberry and Cassis
Frozen Yogurt**

**Ginger Ice Cream
with Rhubarb Sauce**

**Honey-Pistachio
Ice Cream**

**Raspberry-Lemon
Sorbet**

**Chocolate Velvet
Ice Cream**

Blueberry and Cassis Frozen Yogurt

*Ice Cream is great,
but these recipe selections take
you well beyond, into the
world of sorbets, sauces and frozen
yogurt. You can create it all.*

Blueberry and Cassis Frozen Yogurt

Crème de cassis is a delicious liqueur made from black currants. It's often mixed with white wine to make a *kir*, a refreshing aperitif. The deep color and intense flavor of cassis really enhances the blueberries in this frozen yogurt. To make this recipe nonalcoholic, omit the cassis, or substitute an equal amount of blueberry syrup. The recipe calls for whole-milk yogurt, but you can substitute low-fat or nonfat yogurt if you wish; the texture will be a little more grainy and slightly crumbly. You can serve this frozen yogurt with a splash of crème de cassis, whole berries and wafer cookies. Ginger snaps are especially good; serve them whole or crush them to make a crunchy topping.

¾ **cup sugar**
½ **cup crème de cassis**
3 **cups fresh blueberries**
2 **cups plain whole-milk yogurt**

1 **teaspoon grated lemon peel**
2 **tablespoons fresh lemon juice**
⅛ **teaspoon salt**

1. Process sugar in blender at low speed 10 seconds or until powder clings to sides of container and tiny "cakes" start to form in sugar. Add crème de cassis and blueberries; process 20 to 30 seconds or until smooth. Scrape down sides of container once or twice, if necessary.

2. In large bowl, whisk together yogurt, lemon peel, lemon juice and salt. Stir in blueberry puree. Refrigerate several hours or overnight.

3. Make frozen yogurt in ice cream maker according to manufacturer's directions. Transfer to freezer container; let ripen in freezer several hours or overnight before serving.

1½ quarts

Note:

The amount of sugar (also liqueurs, syrups and honey) in an ice cream recipe is one of the factors that determines how soft and "scoopable" it will be. A mixture with too little sugar will freeze very hard and it will have to be warmed before scooping. If there is too much sugar in the mixture, it will never freeze firm enough to scoop.

Ginger Ice Cream with Rhubarb Sauce

Ginger Ice Cream with Rhubarb Sauce

Ginger fans will love this one—creamy and sweet, but intensely flavored whether you use dried or fresh ginger. Ginger and rhubarb are a match made in heaven.

Note:

For Rhubarb Sauce, use fresh rhubarb or frozen rhubarb that has been thawed. Both the Rhubarb Sauce and the toasted almonds can be made in advance. Top each serving of Ginger Ice Cream with 2 to 3 tablespoons of Rhubarb Sauce and 1 tablespoon toasted almonds.

ICE CREAM
- ¼ cup sliced fresh ginger
- 2½ cups whole milk
- 2 cups heavy cream
- 1½ cups sugar
- ¼ teaspoon ground ginger
- 4 egg yolks, lightly beaten
- 1 teaspoon vanilla

RHUBARB SAUCE AND TOASTED ALMONDS
- 4 cups coarsely chopped rhubarb
- 1 cup sugar
- Pinch salt
- 1 cup slivered almonds

1. In large saucepan, heat ginger, milk, cream and sugar over medium heat until milk reaches a low simmer and sugar dissolves. Remove from heat; steep 30 minutes.

2. Stir ground ginger and egg yolks into milk mixture. Stir custard with whisk over medium-low heat until temperature reaches 165°F. Reduce heat to low; continue stirring 5 to 10 minutes, maintaining custard temperature between 165°F and 180°F, until noticeably thicker on back of spoon. Strain custard into container; set aside 20 to 30 minutes, stirring occasionally until custard is cool enough to refrigerate. Stir in vanilla; cover and refrigerate several hours or overnight.

3. Make ice cream in ice cream maker according to manufacturer's instructions. Transfer custard to freezer container. Let custard ripen in freezer several hours or overnight before serving. Serve with Rhubarb Sauce.

4. To prepare sauce, combine rhubarb, sugar and salt in large skillet. Cover and bring to a low simmer. Uncover and simmer 10 to 15 minutes or until sauce is thickened. Cool and refrigerate until ready to serve.

5. To toast almonds, heat small skillet over medium-low heat. Stir in almonds. When golden, pour almonds onto baking sheet to cool. When thoroughly cool, store in airtight container until ready to use. If storing longer than one or two days, wrap well and store in freezer.

1-quart   2 cups

Honey-Pistachio Ice Cream

Honey ice cream is very popular in France, especially in Provence, which is famous for its extraordinary honey. This is a nice alternative to vanilla ice cream, delicious served with all kinds of fruit, especially berries. Choose a dark, flavorful honey, but stick with liquid honey, not creme honey spread.

3	cups whole milk	2	eggs
1	cup heavy cream	2	egg yolks
1	cup honey*	½	cup shelled pistachios, rinsed

1. In large saucepan, combine milk, cream and honey; bring to a simmer over medium-low heat. In medium bowl, combine egg and egg yolks; stir in 1 or 2 cups of the milk mixture. Whisk egg mixture back into saucepan.

2. Stir custard with whisk over medium-low heat until temperature reaches 165°F. Continue stirring, maintaining custard temperature between 165°F and 180°F, 5 to 10 minutes or until noticeably thicker on backside of spoon. Do not let custard boil. Strain custard into large container; set aside 20 to 30 minutes. Stir occasionally until custard is cool enough to refrigerate. Cover and refrigerate several hours or overnight.

3. Make ice cream in ice cream maker according to manufacturer's instructions. Transfer to freezer container; stir in pistachios. Let ice cream ripen in freezer several hours or overnight before serving.

2 quarts

Try one of these variations:

◎ For ice cream with even more exotic Mediterranean flavor, add 2 tablespoons orange flower water when you stir in pistachios.

◎ Or, if you've never tasted herbs in a dessert, try *Honey-Pistachio Ice Cream with Rosemary*. The subtle background flavor is intriguing and delicious. Here's how:

> Change recipe method slightly at step 1 to steep rosemary in warm milk. Place milk, cream, honey and 2 large sprigs of fresh rosemary (or 1 tablespoon of rosemary needles) into saucepan and bring to a simmer. Remove from heat; let steep 30 minutes. Stir together eggs and egg yolks; whisk into milk mixture. Proceed with recipe.

TIP:

*Do not serve honey to infants under 1 year of age. Their immature immune systems sometimes can't cope with the occasional botulism spore that occurs naturally in honey.

Note:

With a custard recipe that contains eggs or egg yolks, cook the custard to 165°F, reducing the heat and then maintaining temperature between 165°F to 180°F. Slowly stir to prevent the eggs from curdling to get the maximum thickening power out of the eggs; this improves texture. It will also destroy any bacteria more effectively than simply cooking to 165°F or 170°F.

Raspberry-Lemon Sorbet

Note:

It's best to start making ice cream or sorbet 1 to 2 days before you want to serve it. Prepare the custard or fruit mixture and refrigerate several hours or overnight. Flavors will mellow and blend, and the texture improves. The ice cream/sorbet mixture should be at 40°F before going into an ice cream maker. Process in your ice cream maker, then let it ripen another 24 hours. After it is thoroughly chilled, it will be ready to scoop.

While this sorbet is very refreshing in the summer months, you can make it anytime of the year because frozen raspberries work very well. If you love limes, use them instead of lemons. Highlight the rich red color by serving scoops of this sorbet in wine or even martini glasses. Garnish each serving with a scoop of fresh whole berries if they are available. Crisp wafer cookies make the perfect finishing touch.

Many sorbet recipes use a simple syrup of sugar and water. It's easier to use superfine sugar, which dissolves quickly. Because superfine sugar can be expensive and hard to find, you might want to make your own; it's simple with a blender or food processor. You can make extra and have it on hand whenever you want a quick-dissolving sugar for dessert sauces, meringues or lemonade.

3 cups fresh raspberries	6 tablespoons fresh lemon juice
1 cup plus 6 tablespoons superfine sugar	1½ teaspoons grated lemon peel
	Dash salt
½ cup water	1½ cups warm water

1. Process raspberries, 6 tablespoons of the superfine sugar and water in food processor 1 to 3 minutes or until smooth. Strain seeds; set aside.

2. In large bowl, combine lemon juice, grated lemon peel, remaining 1 cup superfine sugar, salt and 1½ cups warm. Stir to dissolve sugar. Season with 1 to 2 additional tablespoons of sugar, if desired. Stir in raspberry puree.

3. Chill fruit mixture several hours or overnight. Make sorbet in ice cream maker according to manufacturer's directions; transfer it to freezer container. Let sorbet ripen in freezer several hours or overnight before serving.

1 quart

Chocolate Velvet Ice Cream

This is a rich and velvet-smooth ice cream for special occasions. Choose a good baking chocolate for this recipe, not chocolate chips. (For cookies, they are ideal because they are designed to resist melting and hold their shape. But when chocolate chips are melted, they are a little drier and grainier than regular chocolate.) So many toppings are good on chocolate ice cream—toasted coconut, crushed cookies, candy pieces, marshmallow cream, toasted nuts, caramel sauce and even hot fudge sauce for true chocolate lovers.

1 (6-oz.) block bittersweet chocolate, chopped into ½-inch pieces	6 egg yolks, lightly beaten
1 cup sugar	2 cups whole milk
2 tablespoons unsweetened cocoa	2 cups heavy cream
Dash salt	1 teaspoon vanilla

1. Place chocolate in large bowl; set aside. In medium bowl, beat egg yolks at medium speed until frothy. Set aside.

2. In large saucepan, whisk together sugar, cocoa and salt until well blended. Stir in milk and cream. Bring mixture to a very low simmer over medium-low heat. Pour about half of the mixture over egg yolks; whisk to blend well. Return egg mixture to saucepan.

3. Stir custard with whisk over medium-low heat until temperature reaches 165°F. Continue stirring 5 to 10 minutes, maintaining custard temperature between 165°F and 180°F until noticeably thicker on backside of spoon. Do not let custard boil.

4. Pour custard through strainer into bowl with chocolate. Let sit 2 to 3 minutes or until chocolate is softened; whisk to thoroughly combine melted chocolate with custard. Set aside to cool, stirring occasionally. When mixture is no longer hot, stir in vanilla. Cover and refrigerate several hours or overnight.

5. Make ice cream in ice cream maker according to manufacturer's directions. Transfer ice cream to freezer container; let ripen in freezer several hours or overnight before serving.

About 1½ quarts, 10 to 12 servings

Notes:

When cooking custard, it's important to rely on a thermometer. The relevant temperature range (165°F to 180°F) is below the simmering point; therefore there will be no visual guides to temperature. You can use either an instant-read thermometer or a candy thermometer that can be clipped to side of pan.

For an ice cream party, have a several sizes of scoops on hand. A small scoop (1½ inches wide) can be useful for having smaller tastes of several kinds of ice cream.

Offer several choices and let your guests create their own masterpieces:

◎ To add a little more crunch and even more chocolate flavor to *Chocolate Velvet Ice Cream*, stir in ½ cup of your favorite candy or cookie pieces just before putting ice cream into the freezer to ripen.

◎ For *Chocolate Cinnamon Ice Cream*, add 1½ teaspoons cinnamon, unsweetened cocoa and salt to sugar mixture.

◎ For *Chocolate-Orange Ice Cream*, slightly change recipe method at step 1. Scrub 2 oranges with brush under warm running water. Remove peel with vegetable peeler. Add pieces of peel to saucepan with sugar, cocoa, salt, milk and cream. Bring mixture to a simmer; remove pan from heat. Let steep 30 minutes, allowing orange flavor to permeate ice cream base. After 30 minutes, whisk egg yolks into orange mixture.

Tailgate Party

by Charla Draper

Make this winner of a menu ahead of time and you will be the unanimous MVP at any sporting event.

**Texas
Tailgate Chili**

**Mock
Margarita Punch**

Black Bean Salsa

**Big Ten
Dessert Bars**

**Goal Post
Quesadillas**

Texas Tailgate Chili

It's time to take
a break from hot dogs
and burgers. This great
Tex-Mex menu,
from an awesome chili
to refreshing
mock margaritas,
shows you how
to do it in style.

Texas Tailgate Chili

Texas is tailgate country and a batch of Texas-style chili with cubes of beef makes a hearty lunch before an afternoon of football.

1	ancho chile	2	teaspoons oregano
1	to 1½ cups water	2	teaspoons chili powder
2	tablespoons vegetable oil	1	to 1½ teaspoons ground cumin
2	lb. beef chuck, cut into 1-inch pieces	½	teaspoon salt
1	to 1½ cups chopped onions	⅛	teaspoon freshly ground pepper
¾	cup chopped green bell pepper	1	(28-oz.) can diced tomatoes
1	large garlic clove, minced	1	(15-oz.) can kidney beans
½	cup cold water		

1. In small saucepan, cover ancho chile with hot water; cover and simmer 5 minutes. Remove saucepan from heat.

2. In blender, combine ancho chile and 1½ cups water; process until blended. Set aside.

3. In Dutch oven, heat oil over medium-high heat until hot. Brown meat; remove meat and drippings, reserving 2 tablespoons drippings.

4. Add onions, bell pepper and garlic to Dutch oven; cook over medium heat, stirring occasionally, until onions and bell pepper are tender. Stir in meat, drippings and chili powder. Stir in ancho chile mixture, cumin, salt, pepper, tomatoes and kidney beans; bring to a boil. Reduce heat; cover and simmer 30 minutes.

8 to 10 servings

Note:

To prepare for tailgating, cook this chili in advance and serve from a crockpot or electric skillet at the stadium. Turn the cigarette lighter into an electrical outlet for the crockpot by connecting an adapter available from automotive supply or sporting goods stores.

Mock Margarita Punch

Vitamin-rich fruit and limeade concentrate blend for a Margarita-style cocktail that is alcohol-free.

2	medium kiwi, sliced	1	cup fresh orange juice
1	cup frozen limeade concentrate, thawed	2	cups cold lemon-lime carbonated beverage
2	cups cold water		

1. In blender, process kiwi fruit until smooth*. Pour mixture into 2-quart pitcher. Stir in limeade, water, and orange juice; mix until blended.

2. Just before serving, pour in cold lemon-lime carbonated beverage; mix well. Garnish each serving with lime and orange slices.

6 cups

TIP:

*To use a blender to process the kiwi, spoon 2 to 4 tablespoons limeade or water into container before processing fruit.

Black Bean Salsa

Bean salsa with jicama and cilantro spark any arm-chair coach's training table with a wholesome snack.

1 (15-oz.) can black beans, drained, rinsed	¼ cup chopped fresh cilantro
1 cup chopped tomatoes	½ teaspoon salt
½ cup chopped jicama or celery	¼ teaspoon ground cumin
2 tablespoons chopped red onion	⅛ teaspoon freshly ground pepper
⅔ cup oil-and-vinegar bottled salad dressing	

1. In large bowl, combine beans, tomatoes, jicama and onion; mix gently.

2. In blender, combine salad dressing, cilantro, salt, cumin and pepper; process until smooth. Pour dressing mixture over bean mixture; toss lightly.

3. Chill several hours or overnight. Serve with lime- or cheese-flavored tortilla chips: Garnish with additional chopped fresh cilantro.

About 2 cups

Big Ten Dessert Bars

Big Ten Dessert Bars were made for tailgating! Easy to prepare, ready-to-go, you can bake this cookie to match your team's colors.

TIP:

*To match the colors of your favorite football team, substitute orange marmalade, pineapple, grape or raspberry preserves (or whatever) for the strawberry jam.

BARS
- 6 tablespoons margarine
- ¼ cup sugar
- 1 teaspoon lemon extract
- ¾ cup all-purpose flour
- ¼ cup oat flour
- ½ teaspoon vanilla
- ⅔ cup strawberry jam*
- 1 to ½ teaspoons fresh lemon juice

GLAZE
- ½ cup powdered sugar
- 1 tablespoon fresh lemon juice

1. Heat oven to 375°F.

2. Spray 9-inch square pan with nonstick cooking spray; lightly flour.

3. In small bowl, beat margarine and sugar at medium speed until light and fluffy; blend in lemon extract and vanilla. Gradually add flours; mix until well blended. With lightly greased hands, press into bottom and ½ inch up sides of pan. Bake 10 to 12 minutes or until lightly browned. Cool slightly. Combine jam and lemon juice in small bowl; spread over crust. Bake 10 to 15 minutes or until golden brown; cool

4. For glaze, combine powdered sugar and lemon juice; mix until blended. Drizzle glaze over cooled strawberry layer. To serve, cut into squares.

YIELD: 9 to 12 servings

Goal Post Quesadillas

Kick off the tailgate season with these Southwestern-flavored quesadillas.

1 (10-oz.) can diced tomatoes and green chiles, drained

1 (8.5-oz.) can whole kernel corn, drained

2 tablespoons chopped fresh cilantro

16 (8-inch) flour tortillas*

1 (8-oz.) pkg. shredded Mexican-style natural cheddar cheese

1. In large bowl, combine tomatoes, corn and cilantro; mix well.

2. To assemble quesadilla, cover tortilla with ¼ cup cheese and 2 tablespoons tomato mixture; top with second tortilla. Heat grill. Repeat with remaining tortillas.

3. Place quesadilla on lightly oiled gas grill over low heat or on charcoal grill 4 to 6 inches from low coals. Cook 2 to 4 minutes, turning once, or until quesadilla is lightly browned. Cut in wedges to serve. To prepare in advance, place cooked quesadilla in aluminum foil; reheat on grill. Cut just before serving.

8 servings

TIP:

*Typically made with flour tortillas, this recipe can be made with a 10-inch tortilla and sliced into wedges for serving like pizza. By adding cooked chicken or chorizo sausage, the appetizer quesadilla becomes a heartier main-dish portion.

Creative Kabobs

by Patsy Jamieson

*Simple. Fun. A complete meal.
Everybody loves kabobs, especially
when they're as adventuresome and
out-of-the-ordinary as these ideas.*

**Chicken, Prosciutto
and Sage Kabobs**
Mustard-Shallot Butter

**Rosemary-Scented
Lamb Kabobs**

**North African
Tuna Kabobs**

**Pork Kabobs with
Pineapple-Chipotle
Glaze**

Chicken, Prosciutto and Sage Kabobs

*Pick a kabob recipe and go!
Then, next time you're ready for
kabobs ... pick another one
from this selection— chicken,
lamb, tuna and pork—and go again!*

Chicken, Prosciutto and Sage Kabobs

In addition to flavoring the chicken, a delicate wrapper of sliced prosciutto and sage leaves help keep the meat moist and tender. Prosciutto protects the delicate chicken from the grill's drying heat. Serve these Italian-inspired kabobs with rice pilaf, sautéed spinach and grilled cherry tomatoes.

3	tablespoons fresh lemon juice	¾	cup *Mustard-Shallot Butter* (see below)
3	tablespoons olive oil	4	oz. thinly sliced prosciutto
2	garlic cloves, minced		About 30 fresh sage leaves
½	teaspoon freshly ground pepper		
1¾	lb. boneless skinless chicken breasts, cut into 1¼-inch pieces		

1. In small bowl, whisk together lemon juice, olive oil, garlic and pepper. Place chicken in large bowl. Pour lemon marinade over chicken; turn to coat well. Cover and marinate in refrigerator at least 20 minutes or up to 2 hours, turning chicken occasionally.

2. Meanwhile, prepare Mustard-Shallot Butter.

3. Heat grill.

4. Cut prosciutto slices in half lengthwise, then in thirds crosswise to make 3x1½-inch pieces. Place 1 piece of prosciutto on cutting board; center sage leaf on top. Place chicken piece on sage leaf, then fold up edges of prosciutto to partially enclose chicken. Thread onto 10- or 12-inch skewer. Add 3 or 4 more additional pieces wrapped chicken to skewer. Repeat with remaining prosciutto, sage and chicken to make 6 kabobs.

5. Lightly oil grill rack. Place kabobs on gas grill over medium heat or on charcoal grill 4 to 6 inches from medium coals. Cook covered, turning occasionally, 8 to 10 minutes or until browned and chicken is no longer pink in center. Serve immediately with Mustard-Shallot Butter.

6 servings

Mustard-Shallot Butter

Compound butter sauces are one of the simplest and most satisfying ways to embellish grilled foods. Traditional recipes use all butter, but you can lighten the butter by whipping in an equal proportion of flavorful olive oil, thereby improving the ratio of healthful monounsaturated fats to saturated fats. This butter is also a great way to perk up grilled veal, lamb chops or beef steaks.

¼	cup butter, softened	2	tablespoons finely chopped shallots
¼	cup extra-virgin olive oil	2	tablespoons chopped fresh Italian parsley
2	tablespoons Dijon mustard		
4	teaspoons fresh lemon juice	¼	teaspoon freshly ground pepper

1. In medium bowl, beat butter at medium speed until smooth and creamy. Gradually add oil; beat until well blended. Stir in mustard and lemon juice; continue beating until well blended. Stir in shallots, parsley and pepper. (The butter will keep, covered, in the refrigerator up to 4 days. Serve at room temperature.)

¾ cup

Rosemary-Scented Lamb Kabobs

Notes:

Because lamb leg needs to be carefully trimmed, this Rosemary-Scented Lamb Kabobs recipe makes allowance for loss during trimming. If your meat counter carries cubed, trimmed lamb for kabobs, 1½ lbs. of meat should be enough.

What to do with the lamb trimmings? Make lamb broth by browning trimmings, then simmering in water with several rosemary sprigs and garlic cloves for about 1 hour. Chill, then skim off fat. Freeze for use later in lamb stew or gravy for roast lamb.

Rosemary, garlic and lamb make a magical trio. To accompany these Mediterranean-flavored kabobs, try goat cheese mashed potatoes and steamed green beans.

2 tablespoons chopped fresh rosemary	¾ teaspoon salt
4 garlic cloves, minced	½ teaspoon freshly ground pepper
3 tablespoons olive oil	2¼ lb. boneless leg of lamb, fat and
1 tablespoon red wine vinegar	membrane trimmed, cut into
1 teaspoon Dijon mustard	1¼-inch pieces
½ teaspoon Worcestershire sauce	2 large red bell peppers, seeded, cut into 1¼-inch pieces

1. In small bowl, whisk together rosemary, garlic, oil, vinegar, mustard, Worcestershire sauce, salt and pepper. Place lamb in large bowl. Pour rosemary marinade over lamb; turn to coat well. Cover and marinate in refrigerator at least 30 minutes or up to 2 hours, turning lamb occasionally.

2. Heat grill.

3. On 10- or 12-inch skewer, thread 1 piece lamb, followed by 1 piece bell pepper and another piece of lamb. Continue, alternating lamb and bell pepper, with an additional 4 pieces lamb and 3 pieces bell pepper. Repeat with remaining lamb and bell pepper to make 6 kabobs.

4. Lightly oil grill rack. Place kabobs on gas grill over high heat or on charcoal grill 4 to 6 inches from medium coals. Cover grill and cook, turning occasionally, 6 to 8 minutes or until lamb is thoroughly cooked to slightly pink in center. Serve immediately. Garnished with rosemary sprigs.

 6 servings

GENERAL KABOB TIPS:

◎ If using bamboo skewers, soak them in water for at least 1 hour before threading, to prevent skewers from scorching.

◎ To prevent kabobs from sticking to the grill, make sure that the grill rack is clean. The easiest way to do this is to clean the rack immediately after cooking: While grill is still hot, dip a wire grill brush in water and use it to scrub grill. (Be careful of steam.) Before cooking again, heat grill thoroughly. Lightly oil grill rack just before placing kabobs on the grill. To oil a grill rack, moisten a large piece of folded paper towel with oil, then use it to rub oil over grill rack. (Do not spray cooking spray on a hot grill.)

◎ Some items on kabobs are fragile. Carefully loosen kabobs from grill rack with a wide metal spatula before trying to lift kabobs and turn with tongs.

◎ Keep basic food safety principles in mind. Always marinate perishable food in the refrigerator. Do not use marinade that has been in contact with raw meat, poultry or fish for basting during cooking. If you wish to baste with marinade, reserve some marinade separately for basting. Always place the cooked food on a clean platter.

Rosemary-Scented Lamb Kabobs

North African Tuna Kabobs

North African Tuna Kabobs

Lemon wedges give these kabobs an interesting presentation. When the kabobs are cooked, use raw lemon wedges to squeeze extra lemon juice over the tuna. Serve these kabobs over couscous and accompany with a selection of grilled vegetables.

½   cup chopped fresh cilantro
½   cup chopped fresh Italian parsley
4   garlic cloves, minced
½   cup extra-virgin olive oil
⅓   cup fresh lemon juice
2   teaspoons ground cumin

1½   teaspoons paprika
¾   teaspoon salt
½   teaspoon freshly ground pepper
1¾   lb. tuna steak, dark flesh trimmed,
        cut into 1¼-inch pieces
2   lemons, each cut into 6 wedges

1. In small bowl, whisk together cilantro, parsley, garlic, oil, lemon juice, cumin, paprika, salt and pepper. Reserve ½ cup of marinade.

2. Place tuna in large bowl. Pour remaining marinade over tuna; turn to coat well. Cover and marinate in refrigerator at least 20 minutes or up to 1 hour, turning occasionally. Cover and keep reserved sauce at room temperature.

3. Heat grill.

4. On 10- to 12-inch skewer, thread 1 piece tuna, lemon wedge and an additional 2 pieces tuna. Repeat with remaining tuna and lemon wedges to make 6 kabobs.

5. Lightly oil grill rack. Place kabobs on gas grill over high heat or on charcoal grill 4 to 6 inches from medium coals. Cover grill and cook, turning occasionally, 7 to 9 minutes or until tuna just begins to flake. Serve immediately with reserved sauce.

6 servings

Pork Kabobs with Pineapple-Chipotle Glaze

Chipotle chiles, which are smoked jalapeño chiles, contribute a complex and smoky taste to a barbecue glaze. You can find canned chipotles in Latin markets, specialty stores and some supermarkets. Use these kabobs as the centerpiece of a Latin feast and accompany with black beans and rice, and a crisp slaw made with grated jicama and carrots.

6 slices fresh pineapple	1¾ lb. center-cut boneless pork chops, fat trimmed, cut into 1¼-inch pieces
⅓ cup frozen pineapple juice concentrate, thawed	
2 tablespoons apple cider vinegar	2 bunches scallions, white and light green parts only, cut into 2-inch pieces
2 tablespoons molasses	
4 teaspoons minced, seeded, canned chipotle chiles in adobo sauce	¾ teaspoon salt
1 tablespoon vegetable oil	½ teaspoon freshly ground pepper

1. Cut each pineapple slice into 4 wedges. In small bowl, whisk together pineapple juice concentrate, vinegar, molasses, chiles and oil. Set aside.

2. Heat grill.

3. On 10- to 12-inch skewer, thread 1 piece pork, 1 pineapple wedge, 1 piece of scallion (thread it crosswise) and an additional 1 piece pork. Continue alternating pork, pineapple and scallion with an additional 4 pieces pork, 3 pineapple wedges and 3 scallions. Repeat with remaining pork, pineapple and scallions to make 6 kabobs.

4. Lightly oil grill rack. Season kabobs on all sides with salt and pepper. Place kabobs on gas grill over medium-high heat or on charcoal grill 4 to 6 inches from medium coals. Cover grill and cook, turning occasionally and basting cooked sides with glaze, 8 to 10 minutes or until pork is no longer pink in center. Serve immediately. Garnish with lime wedges and cilantro sprigs.

6 servings

Pork Kabobs with Pineapple-Chipotle Glaze

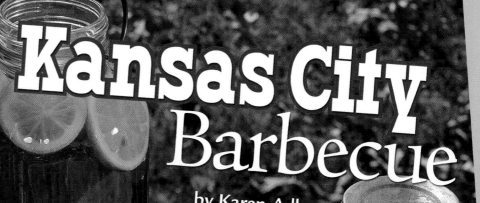

Kansas City
Barbecue
by Karen Adler

Here's the real thing—a no-holds-barred, true blue feast of traditional Kansas City ribs and all the fixings.

Kansas City-Style Barbecued Ribs

menu

Kansas City-Style Barbecued Ribs
Kickin' Kansas City Barbecue Sauce

Tangy Vinegar Cole Slaw

Smokey Barbecued Beans

Dee Conde's Dutch Apple Pie

A grill, good friends and a sunny day make fantastic Kansas City ribs taste even better. Beans, cole slaw and unbelievable apple pie add the finishing touches.

Kansas City-Style Barbecued Ribs

The flavor of celery seeds adds a delicious dimension to these sassy and spicy ribs. At Kansas City barbecue joints, the ribs are served on a platter lined with plain white sandwich bread, with dill pickle slices and extra sauce on the side. Ribs are also good the next day served cold.

RIBS
4 lb. baby back pork ribs

RUB
4 tablespoons sugar
2 tablespoons garlic salt
2 tablespoons freshly ground pepper

2 tablespoons paprika
2 tablespoons celery seed
1 squeeze bottle margarine*
2 cups *Kickin' Kansas City Barbecue Sauce* (see below)
5 to 6 pieces water-soaked wood (apple, oak or cherry)

TIP:
*The squeeze bottle of margarine makes an easy job of keeping the ribs moist during the smoking process.

1. One day before cooking, remove membrane on underside of each rib. (To remove, use needle-nose pliers to grab membrane; pull off in one motion.)

2. In large bowl, combine sugar, garlic salt, pepper, paprika and celery seeds; mix well. Rub mixture onto entire surface of meat. Place ribs in covered container; let flavors blend overnight in refrigerator.

3. In smoker, build indirect charcoal fire with water pan on opposite side. When fire is hot, add about 3 pieces of wood. Maintain 225°F temperature.

4. Place ribs in cooker on rack above water pan (indirect heat); smoke about 2 hours or until meat pulls back from bone about ½ inch. Check wood; if burned down, add additional pieces.

5. Turn ribs; baste with margarine. Cook an additional 1 hour, basting every 10 to 15 minutes. (The more moisture, the better the ribs.) Baste ribs with barbecue sauce during last 30 minutes of cooking.

6 servings

Kickin' Kansas City Barbecue Sauce

Kansas City barbecue sauce is considered too sweet for some. This version adds red pepper and hot sauce to give it a kick. A little more vinegar creates a nice tang.

2 tablespoons butter
1 large onion, finely chopped
4 garlic cloves, minced
2 cups ketchup
2 cups chili sauce
1 cup packed brown sugar
½ cup molasses
½ cup cider vinegar
2 tablespoons Worcestershire sauce

1¼ teaspoons freshly ground pepper
½ teaspoon ground cumin
½ teaspoon paprika
½ teaspoon cayenne pepper
½ teaspoon salt
¼ teaspoon allspice
¼ teaspoon cinnamon
¼ teaspoon ground mace
3 to 4 dashes hot pepper sauce

Note:

Barbecue sauce will keep several weeks in the refrigerator, so enjoy the extra amount this recipe provides.

1. In large saucepan, melt butter over medium-high heat. Sauté onion and garlic until onion is tender.

2. Stir in ketchup, chili sauce, brown sugar, molasses, vinegar, Worcestershire sauce, pepper, cumin, paprika, cayenne pepper, salt, allspice, cinnamon, mace and hot pepper sauce. Reduce heat to medium and simmer, uncovered, 1 hour.

3. Store in airtight jar in refrigerator up to 2 weeks.

6 cups

Smokey Barbecued Beans

Tangy Vinegar Cole Slaw

Tangy Vinegar Cole Slaw

This is a delicious vinegar-based slaw that holds better in the heat of summer than the mayonnaise-base of creamy cole slaws. Napa cabbage is tender and less biting than ordinary cabbage. For a special treat, add 8 ounces of crumbled blue cheese and 4 slices of crisp bacon crumbs to the slaw right before serving.

SLAW
4 cups shredded napa cabbage
1 cup shredded carrots
¼ cup chopped scallions

DRESSING
¼ cup cider vinegar

¼ cup vegetable oil
2 garlic cloves, minced
¼ cup sugar
1 teaspoon celery seed
½ teaspoon salt
½ teaspoon freshly ground pepper

1. In large bowl, combine cabbage, carrots and scallions.
2. In small bowl, whisk together vinegar, oil, garlic, sugar, celery seed, salt and pepper. Pour dressing over slaw; toss and serve.

6 servings

Smokey Barbecued Beans

These are the most delicious barbecued beans you'll ever taste! They're fortified with smoked brisket, barbecued rib meat or smoked sausage.

2 (16-oz.) cans pork and beans
1 medium white onion, chopped
1 cup *Kickin' Kansas City Barbecue Sauce* (page 113)
1 tablespoon dry mustard

1 cup chopped smoked pork, beef and/or sausage
⅛ teaspoon salt
⅛ teaspoon freshly ground pepper

1. Heat oven to 350°F. Spray 2-quart casserole with nonstick cooking spray.

2. In large bowl, combine pork and beans, onion, Kickin' Kansas City Barbecue Sauce, mustard and smoked meat of choice; mix well. Season with salt and pepper.

3. Pour beans into casserole. Bake, uncovered, 1 hour.

6 servings

Dee Conde's Dutch Apple Pie

My mother loves Jonathan apple-picking time in Missouri. A day or two after picking apples she would make these fragrant, juicy pies. Mom organized my father and her 4 daughters to "put by" a half-dozen pies at a time. Mom made the crust, Dad peeled the apples, I made the crumb topping and Nancy sliced apples. Linda and Betsy measured out the cinnamon-sugar and tossed the apples.

CRUST
1 cup all-purpose flour
⅓ cup shortening
½ teaspoon salt
2 to 3 tablespoons ice water

FILLING
¾ cup sugar
1 teaspoon cinnamon
2 tablespoons all-purpose flour

⅛ teaspoon nutmeg
¼ teaspoon salt
7 cups tart apple slices (Jonathan or Granny Smith)

TOPPING
½ cup packed brown sugar
1 cup all-purpose flour
½ cup chilled butter, sliced

1. Heat oven to 400°F.

2. To prepare crust, with pastry blender combine 1 cup flour, ½ cup shortening and ½ teaspoon salt in large bowl until mixture crumbles. Sprinkle in ice water, 1 tablespoon at a time, tossing with fork until flour is moistened. Gather dough into a ball. Roll out on to floured surface. Place dough in 9-inch pie plate; crimp edges.

3. To prepare filling, in small bowl, combine ¾ cup sugar, cinnamon, 2 tablespoons flour, nutmeg and salt. Place apple slices in large bowl; sprinkle with sugar mixture and toss to coat. Heap apples into pie plate.

4. To prepare topping, mix together ½ cup brown sugar and 1 cup flour in large bowl. Add ½ cup butter. With pastry blender, combine until mixture crumbles. Sprinkle crumb topping evenly over apples.

5. Bake 45 minutes. Decrease oven temperature to 350°F. Bake an additional 10 to 15 minutes or until crust and topping are golden brown.

8 servings

Farmers' MARKET

By Nancy Baggett

Spring, summer or fall, this menu helps you make the most of your local farmers' market or produce you've grown on your own. Freshness is the star!

Green Beans with Bacon
and Warm Red Onion Vinaigrette

menu

Green Beans with Bacon and Warm Red Onion Vinaigrette

Farmers' Market Vegetable-Pasta Salad

Hot-Cha-Cha Pan-Grilled Chicken

Summer Vegetable Medley Skillet

Easy Summer Fruit Cobbler

Nothing's left out of this great menu—from a fresh farmers' market salad to a fruity cobbler that tops it all off. It's time to really taste summer.

Green Beans with Bacon and Warm Red Onion Vinaigrette

Hearty and flavorful, this side dish will tempt even those who aren't usually big veggie fans. Although regular green beans work well, the dish is more colorful if they are used in combination with yellow wax beans. The beans can be prepared ahead and reheated.

1½ lb. fresh green beans (or ¾-lb. green beans and ¾-lb. wax beans), trimmed	6 tablespoons red wine vinegar
4 strips thick-sliced bacon	2½ tablespoons sugar
1 tablespoon olive oil	1 teaspoon mustard seed
½ cup finely chopped red onion	½ teaspoon salt
	⅛ teaspoon freshly ground pepper

1. In large skillet, add enough water to just cover beans; bring to a boil over high heat. Boil 6 to 7 minutes or until beans are almost tender. Rinse under cold water in colander; drain well.

2. In same skillet, fry bacon until crisp. Discard all fat except 1 tablespoon. Drain bacon on paper towels; crumble.

3. Add oil and onion to bacon fat in skillet. Cook, stirring constantly, until onion begins to soften. Stir in vinegar, sugar, mustard seed, salt and pepper until sugar dissolves. Simmer 3 to 4 minutes until mixture is reduced by half.

4. Return green beans to skillet. Cook, stirring constantly, just until beans are piping hot and cooked through. Add bacon to beans, tossing to mix. Immediately transfer beans to serving bowl.

4 to 6 servings

Farmers' Market Vegetable-Pasta Salad

An array of vegetables adds crispness and crunch, and a light, zesty lemon and olive oil dressing brings out their fresh flavor. This is a nice change of pace from mayonnaise-based pasta salads and takes great advantage of real, vine-ripened farmers' market tomatoes.

1 cup coarsely diced cucumber	¾ teaspoon dried marjoram
1 cup coarsely diced carrot	¾ teaspoon salt
1 cup coarsely diced cauliflower	¼ teaspoon freshly ground pepper
1 cup coarsely diced celery	⅓ cup extra-virgin olive oil
2 cups elbow macaroni	3 tablespoons fresh lemon juice
3 tablespoons chopped green onion	2½ cups coarsely diced vine-ripened tomatoes
2 tablespoons chopped fresh basil or 1 tablespoon dried	

1. In large bowl, combine cucumber, carrot, cauliflower, celery and pasta.

2. In small bowl, combine onion, basil, marjoram, salt, pepper, oil and lemon juice; stir until well blended. Pour dressing over vegetables; toss to mix. (Salad can be prepared ahead at this point. Cover and refrigerate no longer than 24 hours.) Just before serving, add tomatoes; toss gently. Season with additional salt and pepper, if desired.

5 to 6 servings

Hot-Cha-Cha Pan-Grilled Chicken

Summer Vegetable Medley Skillet

Hot-Cha-Cha Pan-Grilled Chicken

This is a spicy but not fiery-hot dish featuring Tex-Mex flavors. It is particularly good made with crushed chipotle pepper flakes and smoked jalapeños, which not only add heat but a subtle smokey taste as well. If you can't find chipotle flakes in the gourmet spice section or with the dried chiles where you shop, substitute red pepper sauce—the results will still be tempting.

¼ cup reduced-sodium chicken broth	½ teaspoon sugar
1½ tablespoons fresh lime juice	½ teaspoon salt
3 tablespoons canola oil	⅛ teaspoon crushed chipotle
3 tablespoons picante sauce	pepper flakes or ¼ teaspoon
1 teaspoon chili powder	hot pepper sauce
1 teaspoon dried oregano	4 boneless skinless chicken
¾ teaspoon ground allspice	breast halves

1. In small bowl, stir together broth, lime juice, 1 tablespoon of the oil, picante sauce, chili powder, oregano, allspice, sugar, salt and hot pepper sauce. Pour into 2-quart casserole. Add chicken pieces; turn to coat. Cover and refrigerate at least 30 minutes or up to 1 hour.

2. Heat remaining 2 tablespoons oil in medium skillet over high heat until hot. Add chicken pieces; reserve marinade. Reduce heat to medium-high. Cook, turning chicken occasionally 6 to 7 minutes or until browned on all sides. Stir in reserved marinade; bring to a simmer. Reduce heat and simmer chicken, turning occasionally, 10 minutes or until juices run clear. If liquid begins to evaporate from pan, add water 1 teaspoon at a time. Transfer chicken to platter. Spoon pan juices over top. Garnish with sprinkling of cilantro. Serve immediately.

4 servings

Summer Vegetable Medley Skillet

Corn, sweet peppers and summer squash are perennial favorites at farmers' markets, and abundant in home gardens. These vegetables go together beautifully, as in this colorful side dish.

1½ tablespoons butter	½ teaspoon dried marjoram
1 medium onion, finely chopped	¼ teaspoon dried thyme
1 cup diced red and green	½ teaspoon salt plus more to taste
bell peppers	⅛ teaspoon freshly ground pepper
3 cups fresh corn kernels	2 to 3 tablespoons reduced-sodium
2½ cups diced zucchini	chicken broth
2½ cups diced yellow squash	

1. In large skillet, melt butter over medium-high heat. Sauté onion and bell peppers 5 to 6 minutes or until onions begin to brown.

2. Stir in corn, squash, marjoram, thyme, salt and pepper. Increase heat to high, stirring frequently, 5 to 8 minutes or until squash is crisp-tender. Add broth as needed to keep pan from boiling dry.

4 to 6 servings

Easy Summer Fruit Cobbler

This rustic, full-flavored recipe calls for peaches, berries, and plums. Though not often used in cobblers, plums add a welcome fruity flavor, as well as bright color. They are also usually abundant at summer markets, and very economical too.

Note:

This cobbler is a bit easier to make than some because the biscuit mixture requires no rolling out or shaping. Instead, the dough is prepared like a streusel and simply crumbled over the fruit. The topping comes out wonderfully crisp and sweet, providing a pleasing contrast to the tartness of the filling.

FILLING
- ⅔ cup sugar
- 1½ tablespoons cornstarch
- 4 large pitted sliced peaches
- 5 pitted sliced black or red plums
- 1 tablespoon unsalted butter
- 1 cup red raspberries or blackberries
- 1 tablespoon fresh lemon juice

DOUGH
- 1½ cups all-purpose flour
- ½ cup packed brown sugar
- ⅓ cup sugar
- ¾ teaspoon baking powder
- ¼ teaspoon salt
- 5½ tablespoons melted unsalted butter
- 1 large egg, lightly beaten

1. Heat oven to 375°F. Spray 2-quart casserole with nonstick cooking spray.

2. In medium saucepan, combine sugar and cornstarch; mix well. Stir in peaches, plums and butter until well blended. Bring to a simmer over medium-high heat; cook, stirring frequently, about 5 minutes. Stir in berries; remove from heat. Add lemon juice to taste; filling should be tart.

3. In medium bowl, stir together flour, sugars, baking powder and salt. Stir in butter until blended. Add egg; stir with fork until blended. Spread fruit mixture into casserole. Sprinkle clumps of dough mixture evenly over fruit.

4. Set casserole on rimmed cookie sheet. Bake on center rack of oven 35 to 40 minutes or until browned and bubbly. Transfer to wire rack; let cool 15 minutes before serving. Serve with ice cream or whipped cream.

6 to 8 servings

Easy Summer Fruit Cobbler

No Need to Cook

by Mary Evans

Maybe it's too hot outside (and inside) to cook. Or you're too tired from outdoor fun. Here's how you can stay away from the grill, stove or oven, and still eat great.

No Need

menu

Spicy Garlic and Black Bean Dip

Tomato-Cucumber Salsa

Cool and Creamy Smoked Turkey Burrito Wraps

Peach-Lime Pie

Spicy Garlic and Black Bean Dip

Stay cool before, during and after the meal with the ideas in this no-cook menu, starting with the zingy black bean dip and ending with smooth Peach-Lime Pie.

Spicy Garlic and Black Bean Dip

Mashing garlic and salt into a paste changes the garlic's flavor slightly, and thoroughly breaks down the garlic's fibers. This step prevents anyone from biting into pieces of strong, raw garlic hidden in the dip, and allows the flavor to spread throughout.

1	(15-oz.) can black beans, rinsed, drained	2	garlic cloves, minced
¼	cup extra-virgin olive oil	¼	teaspoon salt
1	tablespoon fresh lime juice	½	teaspoon sugar
1	tablespoon chili powder	½	teaspoon hot pepper sauce

1. In food processor combine beans, add oil, lime juice and chili powder. Mash garlic and salt on cutting board using back of fork to form paste. Add garlic paste and sugar to food processor; process until smooth.

2. Add hot pepper sauce to processor; pulse to combine. Refrigerate, covered, until ready to serve. Serve with tortilla chips or raw vegetables.

1½ cups

Tomato-Cucumber Salsa

This tasty salsa is just enough to accompany the Cool and Creamy Smoked Burrito Wraps (page 128). You may decide to double the recipe the next time you're asked to bring something to share at a summer event. Remember to check seasonings any time you make more or less of a recipe. The proportions don't always stay the same.

1	medium tomato, diced	1	tablespoon chopped fresh cilantro
½	cup diced cucumber	1	tablespoon white wine vinegar
2	tablespoons chopped green onion	⅛	teaspoon salt
1	medium jalapeño chile, seeded, chopped	⅛	teaspoon freshly ground pepper

1. In medium bowl, combine tomato, cucumber, green onion, jalapeño, cilantro, white wine vinegar, salt and pepper; stir thoroughly. Refrigerate, covered, until ready to serve.

1½ cups

Cool and Creamy Smoked Turkey Burrito Wraps

This take-off on burritos eliminates any need for cooking. Use precooked smoked turkey from the deli or meat case. We've eliminated the step of combining the burrito or taco seasoning with water and simmering it with the turkey. Instead, tossing the ingredients with the dry mix adds flavor and turns off the heat. Keep any leftover seasoning for future use in a resealable plastic bag.

½	lb. smoked turkey, diced	4	(10-inch) flour tortillas
1	cup (4 oz.) shredded cheddar and Monterey Jack cheese blend	½	cup bottled ranch-style salad dressing
2	tablespoons dry taco seasoning	1½	cups *Tomato Cucumber Salsa* (page 127)
2	cups shredded iceberg lettuce		

1. In medium bowl, combine turkey, cheese and seasoning; toss to coat.

2. Place 4 tortillas on flat surface; divide lettuce among tortillas. Top with smoked turkey mixture. Drizzle each with 2 tablespoons ranch dressing. Fold bottom quarter of tortilla upward over bottom of filling; overlap one side over filling, then other side burrito style. Leave top portion open and spoon in Tomato-Cucumber Salsa.

4 servings

Peach-Lime Pie

A light and crispy pie crust with fresh, tree-ripened peaches is a treat no one can resist. Select peaches that are firm to slightly soft and free from bruises.

CRUST

1¼	cups graham-cracker crumbs
⅓	cup powdered sugar
5	tablespoons melted butter

FILLING

3	medium pitted sliced peaches
¾	cup (6-oz. can) frozen limeade concentrate, thawed
¼	teaspoon almond extract
1	quart vanilla nonfat ice cream, softened

1. In medium bowl, mix together graham-cracker crumbs and powdered sugar. Stir in butter until well blended. Pat over bottom and up sides of 9-inch pie plate. Place in freezer while preparing filling.

2. Puree peaches in food processor. Add limeade and almond extract; process mixture to combine. Add ice cream; pulse to combine. Spoon mixture into prepared crust; freeze several hours or until firm. (Leftover pie may be kept in freezer, covered, several days.)

8 servings

Cool and Creamy Smoked Turkey Burrito Wraps

Peach-Lime Pie

Appetizer Party

by Carole Brown

Sometimes the occasion or its timing doesn't call for a complete meal. Or maybe you just want everyone to mingle and nosh. Either way, here's your solution.

Tapenade with Figs

Marinated Party Olives

Tapenade with Figs

Moutabel (Baba Ghanoush)

Lamb Cocktail Brochettes

Fresh Herb Mayonnaise

This Mediterranean-themed selection—from the olives to the brochettes—will make any and every appetizer lover happy.

Marinated Party Olives

The orange and fennel flavor combo may make this easy recipe one of your favorite party foods. Choose flavorful olives of assorted colors, pitted or not, as you wish. Some good choices would be Spanish Manzanillos, niçoise or other olives from Provence, Italian Gaetas or Sicilians or any of the Mediterranean-style olives from California. Ripe Greek kalamata olives would also be good, but for this party we're going to use them in the Tapenade with Figs.

2	cups mixed olives, rinsed, drained	½	teaspoon dried thyme
1	tablespoon balsamic vinegar	½	teaspoon crushed fennel seed
⅛	teaspoon freshly ground pepper	1	teaspoon minced orange peel
	Dash crushed red pepper	4	tablespoons extra-virgin olive oil
1	tablespoon chopped fresh basil or 1 teaspoon dried		

1. Place olives in medium bowl. In another medium bowl, stir together vinegar, pepper, red pepper, basil, thyme, fennel, orange peel and oil; pour marinade over olives. Cover and mix well.

2. Marinate at room temperature several hours or in refrigerator no longer than 2 days. Remove olives from refrigerator about 30 minutes before serving.

About 2 cups

Note:
One or two minced garlic cloves may be added to the recipe, but the other flavors shine through better if they are not overwhelmed with too much garlic.

Tapenade with Figs

Rich and fruity, this versatile French spread seems to be all about olives. The name "tapenade" comes from the Provençal word for "caper." The caper's unique, slightly bitter flavor is essential to real tapenade.

Since olives are fruit, why not combine them with the fig, another delicious Mediterranean fruit? Figs are not at all a traditional tapenade ingredient, but we love the hint of sweetness they lend. But the real "stealth" ingredient here is anchovies. Even if you are not an anchovy fan, try adding the small amount indicated in this recipe; it stays in the background, but adds a lot to the complexity of flavor. If you love anchovies, give the tapenade a more typical anchovy punch by doubling the amount.

1¼	cups pitted diced kalamata olives	2	tablespoons extra-virgin olive oil
6	dried, pitted, chopped, Mission figs	⅛	teaspoon freshly ground pepper
2	garlic cloves, chopped	2	tablespoons chopped fresh basil or
2	tablespoons capers, drained		1 tablespoon pesto
½	teaspoon anchovy paste or 2 anchovy fillets		

1. In food processor, combine olives, figs, garlic, capers, anchovy paste and oil; pulse until mixture is spreadable but not too finely pureed. Stir in pepper and basil. Cover and refrigerate several hours or overnight.

1½ cups

Note:
Spread the tapenade on crackers, pita wedges or toasted French bread slices. This is an easy recipe to double, and then you'll have leftover tapenade to season pasta sauces or to finish a meat stew. A dollop of tapenade is delicious on top of grilled fish or meats. Refrigerated, tapenade will keep 7 to10 days.

Moutabel (Baba Ghanoush)

The light, smoky flavor of roasted eggplant makes this Middle Eastern spread a real party favorite. The seasoning balance will depend on your taste and the amount of eggplant that you have, so feel free to change the proportions of the ingredients as you wish. Keep the texture of the moutabel slightly chunky, not too pasty-smooth. Serve montabel with wedges of pita bread, baguette slices, crisp lavash or crackers.

Note:

Moutabel is a delicious dip for fresh vegetables. Tomato wedges, crumbled feta cheese and pickled hot or sweet peppers all make tasty garnishes.

2	(2-lb.) purple eggplants	1	teaspoon salt
2	to 3 tablespoons olive oil	⅛	teaspoon freshly ground pepper
⅓	cup sesame tahini	⅛	teaspoon hot pepper sauce or
2	garlic cloves, chopped		cayenne pepper
5	tablespoons fresh lemon juice	⅓	cup extra-virgin olive oil

1. Heat oven to 425°F. Cover 15x10x1-inch baking sheet with aluminum foil.

2. Cut off tops and bottoms of eggplants; cut in half lengthwise. Score flesh with diagonal slashes about halfway through to skin. Brush cut surfaces with oil; place skin side up on baking sheet.

3. Bake on center rack of oven 30 to 45 minutes or until flesh feels very soft when pierced with tip of knife. For grilling, place eggplant, cut sides down, on gas grill over medium heat or on charcoal grill 4 to 6 inches from medium coals. Turn when flesh starts to brown; finish cooking skin side down.

4. Meanwhile, in food processor, combine tahini, garlic, lemon juice, salt, pepper, red pepper sauce and ⅓ cup oil; process until almost smooth, scraping sides of bowl as necessary. Use spoon to scrape cooked flesh out of eggplant skins; add to food processor. Pulse until mixture has slightly chunky texture.

5. Season with salt and pepper. If eggplant seeds remain in mixture, pass Moutabel through strainer. Refrigerate at least 1 hour before serving. To serve, put Moutabel in serving dish; drizzle with a little additional olive oil, if desired. Garnish with chopped parsley and lemon slices.

5½ cups

Moutabel (Baba Ghanoush)

Lamb Cocktail Brochettes with Fresh Herb Mayonnaise

Lamb Cocktail Brochettes
with Fresh Herb Mayonnaise

Cocktail brochettes are an ideal way to offer your guests something hearty but not too filling. Of course, you could substitute beef sirloin, venison, turkey breast, shrimp or even vegetables. Make the Fresh Herb Mayonnaise (below) ahead of time and refrigerate it until you're ready to serve. It makes a great dipping sauce for any brochettes.

1   (2½-to 3-lb.) boneless trimmed leg   ¼   cup extra-virgin olive oil
    or shoulder of lamb, cut into   ⅛   teaspoon freshly ground pepper
    1-inch cubes*   ⅛   teaspoon salt

1. In large bowl, drizzle olive oil over meat. Season meat with pepper and toss to coat. Thread 3 or 4 cubes on each soaked bamboo skewer.** (Brochettes can be prepared up to this point.) Cover meat with plastic wrap and refrigerate up to several hours.

2. To cook brochettes on stove top, heat cast-iron skillet, grill pan or griddle over medium-high heat 1 to 2 minutes or until hot. Lightly season meat with salt. Brush pan lightly with oil. Cook brochettes at least 1 inch apart. Turn skewers once after 1½ to 2 minutes; continue cooking until meat is browned and no longer pink in center.

3. To grill brochettes, heat grill. Cook on gas grill over high heat or on charcoal grill 4 to 6 inches from medium coals, turning once, until browned and no longer pink in center. To broil brochettes, heat broiler. Spread skewers on baking sheet (meat toward center of pan, wooden skewer handles toward the outside edges). Broil about 3 inches from heat until no longer pink in center.

25 brochettes

Fresh Herb Mayonnaise

Fresh herbs star in this quick and easy recipe. Use just one herb or blend several of your favorites. You'll turn bottled mayonnaise into a versatile sauce that can also be served with cold vegetables, sandwiches and salads.

1   cup mayonnaise   3   to 4 tablespoons milk
1   tablespoon Dijon mustard   ⅛   teaspoon salt
4   teaspoons fresh lemon juice   ⅛   teaspoon freshly ground pepper
¼   cup chopped fresh herbs (chives,
    parsley, oregano and thyme)

1. In medium bowl, stir together mayonnaise, mustard, lemon juice and herbs. Stir in enough milk to make a light, soft sauce. Season with salt and pepper.

1½ cups

TIP:

*You will get better yield and the nicest cubes of meat from a leg of lamb, but you can also use the less-expensive shoulder cut. If you want to serve the brochettes on skewers, use 6-inch bamboo skewers. It's easy to eat the meat directly from a skewer of that size.

TIP:

**Soak bamboo skewers in water for about 20 minutes if you plan to cook them under the broiler or on the grill. If you prefer, use larger metal skewers and transfer the cooked meat to a platter with toothpicks on the side for spearing.

Note:

This mayonnaise sauce can be made several hours or even one day ahead.

A Family Picnic

by Beatrice Ojakangas

*Forget about sandwiches,
chips and store-bought cookies.
For your next picnic opportunity,
make these ideas ahead of time
and go in delicious style.*

Crusty Cashew Chicken

A Family

menu

Crusty Cashew Chicken

Herbed German-Style Potato Salad

Tomato, Broccoli and Olive Salad

Orange Chocolate Chip Cake

*These recipes—
all variations on old favorites—
will delight any and every picnic-er.
Tote the food in a cooler,
but remember that most of the flavors
are best at room temperature.*

Crusty Cashew Chicken

Delicious hot or cold, this is an easy oven-fried chicken. The recipe is easily multiplied to feed a crowd.

½ cup dry bread crumbs
½ cup finely crushed, salted, roasted cashews
½ cup (2 oz.) freshly grated Parmesan cheese
½ teaspoon paprika

¼ teaspoon freshly ground pepper
1 egg, beaten with 2 tablespoons water
1¼ lb. boneless chicken skinless breast halves
6 chicken drumsticks

1. Heat oven to 350°F. Cover 15x10x1-inch pan with aluminum foil. Spray foil with nonstick cooking spray.

2. In large bowl, combine bread crumbs, cashews, cheese, paprika and pepper; mix well.

3. Dip chicken pieces into egg mixture, then roll in crumb mixture. Arrange chicken on pan about 2 inches apart.

4. Bake 45 minutes to 1 hour or until meat is no longer pink in center and juices run clear. To serve cold, let cool slightly, cover loosely with foil and refrigerate until well chilled.

About 6 servings

Herbed German-Style Potato Salad

Potatoes simmered in chicken broth gain a rich flavor in this version of German potato salad. This is a perfect salad to make a day or two in advance for convenience, but for the best flavor be sure to bring the salad to room temperature before serving.

6 boiling potatoes, peeled
1½ cups reduced-sodium chicken broth
2 green onions, trimmed, thinly sliced
1 tablespoon German-style mustard
¼ cup cider vinegar

½ cup olive oil
1 teaspoon salt
⅛ teaspoon freshly ground pepper
1 bunch finely chopped parsley
½ cup finely minced fresh chives

1. Cut potatoes into ¼-inch slices and place in medium pot. Add broth; bring to a boil over medium-high heat. Reduce heat to medium, cover and simmer about 15 minutes or until potatoes are fork-tender.

2. In large bowl, combine onions, mustard, vinegar, oil, salt and pepper. Add potatoes; blend gently. Cover and refrigerate at least 6 hours or overnight. Drain off excess liquid. Fold in parsley and chives. Serve at room temperature.

6 servings

Tomato, Broccoli and Olive Salad

Tasty and colorful, you can make this salad a day ahead, if you wish. Once again, the flavors are best at room temperature.

2 cups broccoli florets	1 tablespoon chopped fresh basil
4 ripe tomatoes	or 1 teaspoon dried
1 cup pitted kalamata olives, drained	½ teaspoon dried oregano
¼ cup red wine vinegar	½ cup extra-virgin olive oil
2 green onions, sliced	

1. In large saucepan, bring just enough water to cover broccoli to a rolling boil over medium-high heat. Boil 1 to 2 minutes or just until broccoli is blanched. Drain and plunge quickly in ice-cold water. Drain thoroughly.

2. Cut tomatoes into 6 wedges each. In large bowl, combine broccoli, tomatoes and olives. In small bowl, whisk together vinegar, onions, basil, oregano and oil. Pour over the tomato-broccoli mixture; stir gently to coat. Cover and marinate 2 hours or up to 24 hours, stirring once or twice. Serve at room temperature.

6 servings

Orange Chocolate Chip Cake

Orange and chocolate combine in this syrup-soaked cake to make this a favorite for a picnic dessert ... or a coffee break snack.

Note:

Moist and delicious, this cake keeps incredibly well. Freeze squares of this cake, if you have any left, and reheat in the microwave for a few seconds to make an appealing impromptu dessert any time.

CAKE	¾ teaspoon baking powder.
¾ cup sugar	1 cup semisweet chocolate chips (6 oz.)
¾ cup butter	¾ cup buttermilk
2 eggs	
Grated peel of 1 orange	**SYRUP**
2 cups all-purpose flour	¾ cup fresh orange juice
¾ teaspoon baking soda	¾ cup sugar

1. Heat oven to 350°F. Spray 9-inch square cake pan with nonstick cooking spray.

2. In large bowl, beat sugar and butter at medium speed until smooth. Add eggs; beat at medium speed until mixture is light and lemon colored. Stir in grated orange peel.

3. In another large bowl, stir together 2 cups flour, baking soda and baking powder. Add 1 tablespoon of the flour mixture to chocolate chips; mix well. Add flour mixture to sugar mixture alternately with the buttermilk; mix until smooth batter forms. Fold in chocolate chips; pour into pan. Bake 30 to 40 minutes or toothpick inserted near center comes out clean.

4. Meanwhile, combine orange juice and sugar in small saucepan. Stir and bring to a boil over medium-high heat. Stir until sugar is dissolved. Pour boiling hot glaze evenly over cake as soon as it is removed from oven. Cool thoroughly in pan. Cut cake into squares to serve.

9 servings

Tomato, Broccoli and Olive Salad

Orange Chocolate Chip Cake

Vegetables, Vegetables

by Lisa Golden Schroeder

You don't need to be a vegetarian to appreciate this meal, which capitalizes on the bounty of summer vegetables and fruits in your garden or at the market.

menu

Fire-Roasted Asparagus and Portobello Mushroom Pasta

Grilled Pesto Corn

Spicy Black-Eyed Pea Relish

Blueberry Cheesecake Frozen Yogurt

Fire-Roasted Asparagus and Portobello Mushroom Pasta
Grilled Pesto Corn

You really don't need meat to make a meal complete. And after this meatless meal, you won't leave the table feeling shortchanged.

Fire-Roasted Asparagus
and Portobello Mushroom Pasta

Grilling is not only for meat-eaters! The cornucopia of summer harvest is only enhanced by a little smoke and fire. Here, asparagus spears and mushrooms take center grill, roasted until tender and golden. Toss with any preferred combination of fresh herbs—but rosemary, sage and parsley are especially good.

3	to 4 tablespoons olive oil	1½	teaspoons minced fresh rosemary
6	medium plum tomatoes, halved	1	teaspoon salt
8	large garlic cloves, halved	1	(12-oz.) pkg. linguine
1	lb. fresh asparagus	⅓	cup toasted pine nuts or coarsely
12	oz. portobello mushrooms		chopped walnuts
	(about 6 large caps)	¼	cup (1 oz.) freshly grated Asiago
⅓	cup chopped fresh parsley		or Romano cheese
1	tablespoon thinly sliced fresh sage	⅛	teaspoon freshly ground pepper

1. Heat grill.

2. Lightly brush tomatoes, garlic, asparagus and mushrooms with olive oil. Place 12x18-inch piece of heavy-duty aluminum foil on grill. Place tomatoes and garlic on foil; cover and cook on gas grill over medium heat or on charcoal grill 4 to 6 inches from medium coals 4 minutes, turning once, until tomatoes are soft and slightly charred. Transfer to large bowl.

3. Remove foil from grill. Place asparagus and mushrooms directly on grill. Cover and cook 6 to 7 minutes, turning once, until tender and browned. Remove from grill; place in bowl with tomatoes and garlic.

4. Meanwhile, cook pasta according to package directions; drain well. Place in another large bowl. Mince cooked garlic and coarsely chop asparagus and mushrooms; add to pasta. Add parsley, sage, rosemary, salt and remaining olive oil to pasta. Gently toss until well mixed. Serve pasta hot, sprinkled with nuts and cheese. Season with pepper.

6 servings

Grilled Pesto Corn

Nothing symbolizes summer more than fresh sweet corn. Grilling it in its own husk, spread with seasonings, is simply elegant and fun! Softened butter and fresh herbs can be used, but here prepared basil pesto is pressed into service.

6	large ears corn, on husks
⅓	cup pesto

1. Heat grill.

2. Carefully peel back corn husks, but do not remove. Remove and discard corn silk. Rinse corn; pat dry. Using fingers, spread pesto evenly over each ear of corn. Carefully fold husks back. Secure husk tops with cotton or jute kitchen string.

3. Place corn on gas grill over medium heat or on charcoal grill 4 to 6 inches from medium coals. Cover and cook about 25 minutes, turning occasionally, until tender. To serve, remove string and peel back husks. Squeeze lemon juice over corn, if desired.

6 servings

Note:

Put corn on the grill before you begin grilling the vegetables for the pasta. The ears of corn will stay warm, still wrapped in their husks and covered with foil, while the rest of the meal grills.

Spicy Black-Eyed Pea Relish

Earthy-tasting "cowpeas" and collard greens are a classic New Year's Day menu offered in many Southern homes. But black-eyed peas also make a wonderful base for a chilled salad—distinctive in appearance and high in protein. Smoky chipotle chiles and radish add some zing to this tangy sweet salad. Make this salad up to one day before serving, as the flavors become even better.

TIP:

*Chipotles are smoked jalapeño chiles; look for them in small cans, where they come marinated in a spicy tomato sauce.

2 (15-oz.) cans black-eyed peas, rinsed, drained	2 chipotle chiles in adobo sauce, finely chopped*
1 medium yellow or red bell pepper, diced	2 tablespoons cider vinegar
½ cup chopped radish	1 tablespoon sugar
½ cup diced red onion	1 tablespoon olive oil
½ cup chopped fresh cilantro	2 teaspoons Dijon mustard

1. In large bowl, combine peas, bell pepper, radish, onion, cilantro and chiles. Toss gently to mix.

2. In small bowl, combine vinegar, sugar, oil and mustard; whisk until well blended. Pour over salad; gently mix until salad is evenly coated. Cover and refrigerate until ready to serve.

6 servings

Blueberry Cheesecake Frozen Yogurt

Making your own cool confections is especially appealing during warm weather. What could provide more old-fashioned entertainment than the anticipation of freshly made frozen treats? Scoop this deceptively rich blueberry concoction into cones for the kids; make it more indulgent with a drizzle of blueberry sauce or some fresh berries, or serve over wedges of angel food cake for the older kids-at-heart!

CHEESECAKE
1 (8-oz.) pkg. Neufchâtel light cream cheese, softened
⅔ cup sugar
1½ cups fresh blueberries, lightly mashed
2 cups vanilla-flavored yogurt
1 tablespoon fresh lemon juice

1 teaspoon grated lemon peel
½ teaspoon ground cinnamon

FRESH BLUEBERRY COULIS
2 cups fresh blueberries
¼ cup honey
¼ cup crème de cassis or black currant syrup
2 tablespoons fresh lemon juice

1. In large bowl, beat cream cheese and sugar at medium speed until smooth and creamy. Add 1½ cups blueberries, yogurt, lemon juice, lemon peel and cinnamon; beat to blend. Chill mixture 30 minutes.

2. Pour mixture into ice cream maker (1-quart capacity or larger). Freeze according to manufacturer's directions until mixture is firm enough to scoop.

3. Serve softly frozen or freeze at least 3 hours or up to 1 week. Serve drizzled with warm Fresh Blueberry Coulis.

4. To prepare coulis, combine 2 cups blueberries, honey, crème de cassis and lemon juice in medium saucepan. Bring to a simmer; cook and stir 3 to 5 minutes or until berries burst and sauce thickens. (Sauce can be made up to one day ahead; refrigerate sauce and gently reheat before serving.)

1 quart

Blueberry Cheesecake Frozen Yogurt

Summer Tea Party

by Mary Evans

Here are the flavor-filled ideas you need to create a summer tea party that goes way beyond the ordinary.

Iced Jasmine-Almond Tea
Iced Strawberry-Mint Tea
Iced Lemon-Ginger Tea

menu

Iced Jasmine-Almond Tea

Iced Strawberry-Mint Tea

Iced Lemon-Ginger Tea

Iced Chai

Curried Chicken
Salad Sandwiches

Coconut Shrimp
Sandwiches

Cucumber,
Avocado and Salmon
with Sticky Rice
on Sesame Crackers

Savory
Cheddar-Chive
Scones with
Virginia Ham

Individual
Fresh Fruit Tarts

*Tea need not be boring:
the four icy ideas
that follow are proof!
They go perfectly
with the sandwiches, scones,
spread and fruity tarts.
Make a few, or make it all!*

Iced Jasmine-Almond Tea

Jasmine tea is made by combining green tea leaves with jasmine blossoms. You'll love the soothing aroma and flavor.

8   cups water
3   tablespoons loose jasmine tea or
        8 jasmine tea bags

2   tablespoons honey
½   teaspoon almond extract

1. In large saucepan, bring water to a boil over high heat. Remove from heat; stir in tea. Steep 10 minutes; strain into large bowl.

2. Stir in honey until dissolved; stir in almond extract. Let cool to room temperature; refrigerate, covered, until ready to serve. Serve in tall, ice-cube-filled glasses.

8 cups

Note:

Green teas, such as this one, contain very little caffeine and provide healthful antioxidants.

Iced Strawberry-Mint Tea

This iced tea shouts "summer" with its refreshing minty taste underlined with berries. The syrup in the frozen strawberries adds just the right amount of sweetness.

8   cups water
8   orange pekoe tea bags
1   (10-oz.) pkg. frozen whole
        strawberries in syrup, thawed

1   cup chopped fresh mint

1. In teakettle or large saucepan, bring water to boil over high heat. Place tea bags, strawberries and syrup and mint leaves in large bowl; mix well. Pour boiling water over strawberry mixture; steep 5 minutes. Strain; let cool to room temperature.

2. Pour into pitcher; add 2 cups ice cubes. Serve in tall, ice-cube-filled glasses.

10 cups

Iced Lemon-Ginger Tea

This tea is more properly considered an infusion, as herbal teas really contain no tea leaves. Instead, they are mixtures of herbs and flavorings that are steeped in the same manner as regular teas.

7   cups water
6   pieces fresh ginger, unpeeled
        (¼-inch thick)

4   lemon-flavored herbal tea bags
1   (12-oz.) can frozen lemonade
        concentrate, thawed

1. In medium saucepan, bring 4 cups water and ginger to a boil over medium heat. Reduce heat to low; simmer 10 minutes. Remove from heat. Add tea bags and steep 5 minutes; strain.

2. Add remaining 3 cups water and lemonade concentrate; let cool to room temperature. Pour into pitcher; add 2 cups ice cubes. Serve in tall, ice-cube-filled glasses.

10 servings

Iced Chai

Chai means *tea* in India. We've used traditional elements here, but made brewing convenient by using ground spices rather than the traditional whole form.

7 cups water	¼ teaspoon freshly ground pepper
¾ teaspoon ground cardamom	1 (14-oz.) can nonfat sweetened
¼ teaspoon ground cloves	condensed milk
¼ teaspoon ground ginger	8 orange pekoe tea bags

1. In large saucepan, bring water to boil over high heat. Remove from heat; stir in cardamom, cloves, ginger and pepper. Add tea bags; steep 5 minutes. Remove bags; let cool to room temperature, about 45 minutes.

2. Strain through paper towel-lined strainer into pitcher. Stir in sweetened condensed milk; refrigerate, covered, until ready to serve. Serve in tall, ice-cube-filled glasses.

8 cups

Curried Chicken Salad Sandwiches

The English invented mango chutney during their colonial rule in India as a way to duplicate exotic flavors at home. They did the same with curry powder. Use this chicken salad for regular sandwiches, too, or on a lettuce leaf with a wedge of melon for an elegant luncheon dish.

1 cup cooked finely chopped chicken	1 teaspoon curry powder
¼ cup finely chopped celery	⅛ teaspoon salt
2 tablespoons chopped green onion	10 slices raisin, raisin nut or white
2 tablespoons mango chutney	bread, crusts trimmed
2 tablespoons mayonnaise	5 teaspoons butter, softened

1. In medium bowl, mix together chicken, celery, green onion, chutney, mayonnaise, curry powder and salt.

2. Spread bread slices with butter; spread chicken salad mixture over butter on 5 slices. Top with remaining 5 slices. Cut each sandwich into 4 squares or triangles.

20 sandwiches

Curried Chicken Salad Sandwiches

Coconut Shrimp Sandwiches

The inspiration for this recipe comes from combining the flavors of the popular fried coconut shrimp appetizer with the more customary English potted shrimp. Buttering the bread slices helps keep the filling from turning the bread soggy.

1	cup shelled deveined small shrimp	⅛	teaspoon ground ginger
1	(3-oz.) pkg. cream cheese, softened		Pinch cayenne pepper
¼	cup coconut flakes	10	slices white bread, crusts removed
1	tablespoon cocktail sauce	5	teaspoons butter
⅛	teaspoon salt		

Note:

If you're making the sandwiches several hours ahead, store them well-covered in the refrigerator to prevent drying.

1. Reserve 10 shrimp; set aside. Place remaining shrimp in food processor; coarsely chop. Add cream cheese, coconut, cocktail sauce, salt, ginger and cayenne pepper; finely chop.

2. Spread one side of each slice white bread with butter. Spread shrimp mixture over 5 slices; top with remaining 5 slices, butter side inward. Cut each sandwich into 4 squares or triangles. Cut reserved shrimp in half lengthwise; center on top of each square or triangle.

20 sandwiches

Cucumber, Avocado and Salmon with Sticky Rice on Sesame Crackers

Use your imagination when creating finger sandwiches for teas. These bite-size morsels take their inspiration from Japanese sushi, and would be equally at home on an hors d'oeuvre tray.

1	cup water	⅓	(3-oz.) pkg. thinly sliced lox-style smoked salmon
½	teaspoon salt		
½	cup small-grain rice, such as calrose or sushi	¼	avocado, cut into ½-inch strips
1	tablespoon rice vinegar	20	thin slices cucumber
		20	thin sesame crackers

1. In small saucepan, bring water and salt to a boil over medium-high heat. Reduce heat to low. Add rice; cover and cook 15 minutes. Remove from heat; leave covered an additional 15 minutes. Stir in rice vinegar. Let cool.

2. Place 1 (12x10-inch) piece plastic wrap on counter. Place rice on plastic wrap. Using another piece of plastic wrap, flatten rice into 10x6-inch rectangle. Remove top layer of plastic wrap.

3. Arrange salmon slices to cover center of rice in 10x4-inch strip, leaving 1-inch border of rice on each of long sides. Place strips of avocado down center of salmon.

4. Using plastic wrap as guide, gently but firmly roll rice around salmon and avocado to form 10-inch log. Use plastic wrap to press rice log together firmly; place in freezer 45 minutes or until exterior is slightly frozen. Place cucumber slices on top of crackers.

5. Slice log thinly into 20 slices; place each slice onto cucumber topped cracker. Thaw 10 to 15 minutes at room temperature before serving. Store, covered, in refrigerator.

10 servings

Savory Cheddar-Chive Scones
with Virginia Ham

Individual Fresh Fruit Tarts

Savory Cheddar-Chive Scones with Virginia Ham

Scones can be made in many shapes and textures. Some resemble our more familiar American biscuits, as do these.

2½ cups all-purpose flour
1½ teaspoon baking powder
½ teaspoon baking soda
½ teaspoon salt
5 tablespoons unsalted butter, cut into ½-inch pieces
1 cup (4 oz) shredded extra-sharp cheddar cheese

1 cup buttermilk
1 egg
⅓ cup chopped fresh chives
¼ cup butter, softened
8 oz. sliced Virginia ham, halved

Note:

Try this recipe without the ham, as a biscuit accompaniment to your favorite chicken dinner.

1. Heat oven to 425°F. Line baking sheet with parchment paper; set aside.

2. In medium bowl, stir together flour, baking powder, baking soda and salt. With pastry cutter or tips of fingers, cut butter into flour until mixture crumbles; stir in shredded cheese. In small bowl, beat buttermilk and egg together at medium speed until frothy; stir in chives. Stir buttermilk mixture into flour mixture to form coarse dough.

3. Turn dough out onto lightly floured surface and gently knead 6 to 8 times to combine. Roll dough out to about ¾ inch thickness. Cut dough using 2-inch cutter; place on baking sheet. Bake 12 to 15 minutes or until lightly browned. Remove to wire rack; let cool.

4. Cut scones in half cross-wise; spread thinly with butter. Divide ham among bottom halves of scones; top with remaining halves.

20 scones

Individual Fresh Fruit Tarts

Vary this recipe by using your favorite jam instead of marmalade. Any small fresh fruit works well here; try grapes or raspberries instead.

½ (17.3-oz.) pkg. frozen puff pastry, thawed
1½ teaspoons sugar

10 teaspoons orange marmalade
10 fresh strawberries, halved
20 fresh blueberries

1. Heat oven to 350°F. Line baking sheet with parchment; set aside.

2. Roll pastry on lightly floured surface into 12x10-inch rectangle. Cut 10 circles from pastry using 2½-inch round cutter; place on baking sheet. Inside each circle, cut another circle using a 2-inch round cutter. Run finger dipped in water around edge of inner cut circle. Carefully lift edge of half of outer ring of pastry and invert to line up with outer edge of inner circle on the other side. Lift other half of outer ring and invert to line up with other edge to form case. (The overlapping portions form a decorative curlicue on each side.) Gently press together to seal. Repeat with remaining pastry. Prick inner area with tines of fork every ¼-inch. Sprinkle with sugar; bake 20 to 25 minutes or until crisp and brown. Let cool on wire rack.

3. Before serving, fill each tart with ½ teaspoon marmalade. Top with half of one strawberry and 2 blueberries.

10 tarts

party
for a crowd

by Beatrice Ojakangas

Graduation party, family reunion, whatever the occasion ... here's a great tasting way to feed a crowd in real style.

menu

Tuna and Penne Pasta
with Peppers and Chives

Grilled Ratatouille
with Olive Oil and Herbs

Mediterranean
Vegetables

Porketta Pesto
Sandwiches
with
Tomatoes
and Provolone

Layered Strawberry
and Raspberry
Sponge Cake
with Cream

Tuna and Penne Pasta with Peppers and Chives

Ham sandwiches and
potato salad have their place,
but when you're ready
to treat a larger get-together
with something a little more special,
turn to the delights of this menu.

tuna and penne pasta with peppers and chives

Grill tuna steaks (fresh are best) to make this appealing platter main dish. The recipe can be easily multiplied for an even larger crowd. If you substitute canned tuna, select chunk style tuna for the most attractive presentation.

3 (6-oz.) tuna steaks or 2 (12-oz.) cans chunk-style tuna, drained	1 (12-oz.) jar coarsely chopped roasted red bell peppers, drained
½ teaspoon toasted sesame oil, if desired	¾ cup pitted ripe olives, preferably Mediterranean style
4 tablespoons extra-virgin olive oil	2 tablespoons balsamic vinegar
1 teaspoon coarse (kosher) salt	½ teaspoon salt
1 lb. penne	¼ teaspoon crushed red pepper
1 (14-oz.) can baby corn cobs, drained, rinsed	2 tablespoons chopped fresh chives
	2 tablespoons chopped fresh Italian parsley

1. Heat grill. Brush tuna steaks on both sides with sesame oil and 1 tablespoon of the olive oil; sprinkle with salt. Place tuna on gas grill over medium-high heat or on charcoal grill 4 to 6 inches from medium coals. Grill 4 to 5 minutes or until fish flakes easily with fork. Transfer onto cutting board and cut into 1-inch pieces.

2. Drizzle pasta with remaining oil; toss until well coated. Stir in corn, peppers, olives, vinegar, salt and crushed pepper; toss until blended. Add tuna; sprinkle with chives and parsley.

6 to 8 servings

grilled ratatouille with olive oil and herbs

Perfect for an outdoor party, the vegetables of classic ratatouille are perfect for grilling. Once grilled, cut them into bite-size pieces and dress with a tomato vinaigrette.

1 large eggplant	8 to 10 whole portobello mushrooms
⅛ teaspoon salt	¾ cup olive oil
1 large sweet onion, sliced	1 large tomato, peeled, seeded, chopped
2 zucchini or yellow crookneck squash, halved lengthwise	3 tablespoons white balsamic vinegar
2 red, yellow or green bell peppers, seeded, cut crosswise into 1-inch-thick rings	2 garlic cloves, minced
	½ teaspoon freshly ground pepper
	½ cup chopped fresh basil

1. Trim eggplant; cut crosswise into slices about ½-inch thick. Sprinkle both sides of each slice with salt. Spread on paper towel; drain 1 hour.

2. Heat grill.

3. Rinse eggplant to remove salt; pat dry. Set aside. Brush onion, zucchini, bell peppers and mushrooms with ½ cup of the oil; place vegetables on gas grill over medium heat or on charcoal grill 4 to 6 inches from medium coals. Grill, turning once, 10 to 12 minutes or until vegetables are tender. Remove from grill; let cool. Cut into bite-size pieces; place in large bowl.

4. Whisk together remaining ¼ cup oil, tomato, vinegar, garlic, salt and pepper; add to vegetables. Toss gently to combine. Sprinkle with basil. Serve at room temperature.

6 to 8 servings

mediterranean vegetables

Vegetables in season are the most delicious. If you are not a gardener visit the local farmers' market for fresh produce. This salad looks pretty when offered on a large, shallow platter.

DRESSING
½ cup olive oil
⅓ cup red wine vinegar
2 teaspoons chopped fresh oregano
   or ¾ teaspoon dried
1 teaspoon salt
2 garlic cloves, minced

SALAD
2 small cucumbers, diced
4 tomatoes, seeded, diced
1 sweet red onion, thinly sliced,
   separated into rings

2 (6-oz.) jars marinated artichoke
   hearts
8 small red potatoes, steamed, quartered
1 lb. young green beans, trimmed,
   steamed

GARNISH
¾ cup pitted Greek or ripe olives
1 cup (4 oz.) crumbled feta cheese
2 tablespoons capers, drained
2 tablespoons chopped fresh parsley

1. In medium bowl, combine olive oil, vinegar, oregano, salt and garlic; cover and shake until blended. Set aside.

2. In large bowl, combine cucumbers, tomatoes, onions and artichoke hearts, including marinade. Spoon mixture into large, shallow platter. Arrange potatoes and green beans around cucumber mixture; drizzle with salad dressing.

3. Before serving, garnish with olives, cheese and capers. Sprinkle with parsley. Serve at room temperature.

6 to 8 servings

porketta pesto sandwiches with tomatoes and provolone

The herb, garlic and peppered roast loin of pork is a classic in the Mediterranean. Typically, the meat is cooked over an open wood fire. Delicious hot off the grill, this pork is even better the second day, making it a perfect choice for fill-your-own sandwich buns. Offer the thinly sliced meat on a platter along with pesto for spreading on split hard rolls or kaiser buns, sliced provolone and vine-ripened tomatoes.

15 garlic cloves
½ cup fresh rosemary or 3
   tablespoons dried
1 tablespoon coarse (kosher) salt
1½ tablespoons freshly ground pepper

2 tablespoons olive oil
1 (4- to 6-lb.) boneless pork loin
12 hard rolls, split
6 tablespoons pesto
3 large beefsteak tomatoes, quartered

1. In food processor, coarsely chop garlic, rosemary, salt and pepper. Slowly drizzle in oil.

2. Wash meat and pat dry. Rub with garlic mixture, coating evenly. Wrap tightly in aluminum foil and refrigerate overnight. Remove from refrigerator 1 hour before roasting. Unwrap and place on roasting pan.

3. Heat oven to 325°F. Insert meat thermometer into center of meat. Bake 1½ hours. Increase heat to 400°F. Bake an additional 15 minutes.

4. Let roast cool to room temperature; slice thinly. Spread hard rolls with pesto and top with meat and one slice of tomato.

4 servings

Mediterranean Vegetables

Porketta Pesto Sandwiches with Tomatoes and Provolone

Layered Strawberry and Raspberry Sponge Cake with Cream

layered strawberry and raspberry sponge cake with cream

The sponge cake is incredibly simple to make, and can be prepared several days ahead of time. Split and fill the layers a few hours before serving to allow the cake to absorb juices from the berries.

note:

If you have an abundance of fresh berries, serve a spoonful on the side of a slice of this cake.

CAKE
- 6 large eggs, room temperature
- 1½ cups granulated sugar
- 1 teaspoon vanilla
- 1½ cups all-purpose flour
- ¼ teaspoon salt

FROSTING
- 2 cups heavy cream
- 4 tablespoons powdered sugar
- ½ cup raspberry liqueur or light rum
- 2 cups sliced fresh strawberries
- 1 cup fresh raspberries

1. Heat oven to 350°F. Line bottom of 2 (9-inch) round cake pans with parchment paper rounds.

2. In large bowl, beat eggs at medium speed until frothy. Increase speed to high and slowly add sugar and vanilla. Reduce speed to low; sift in flour and salt. Mix just until blended.

3. Divide batter between pans and smooth tops of cakes. Bake 25 minutes or until top springs back when touched. Remove from oven and cool in pans on wire rack. Loosen edges and remove cakes from pans. Store in refrigerator.

4. Split each cake into 2 parts using long, thin knife forming 4 layers.

5. In medium bowl, beat cream at medium speed until stiff peaks form. Stir in powdered sugar.

6. Place half of 1 layer on plate. Drizzle with 1 to 2 tablespoons liqueur. Top with half of the strawberries. Spread with ½ cup of the whipped cream. Top with second half of first layer. Drizzle again with liqueur. Spread with raspberries and ½ cup whipped cream. Top half of the second layer; drizzle with liqueur. Spread with remaining strawberries and ½ cup whipped cream. Top with remaining half cake layer; drizzle with remaining liqueur. Spread with remaining ½ cup whipped cream.

12 servings

Fresh & Fabulous Brunch

by Carole Brown

Dinner, or an evening party, isn't the only time you can enjoy a warm-weather get-together. How about an outdoor brunch?

Potato, Red Bell Pepper and Onion Frittata

Fresh and Fabulous are the watchwords here. Of course, you'll have to do the preparation inside, but then you'll have plenty of time to get outside and enjoy the festivities.

Potato, Red Bell Pepper and Onion Frittata

This open-faced omelet is a practical way to serve several people at once. To save time, cook the onion, pepper and potatoes in advance. When you're ready to make the omelet, heat the vegetables in the skillet, pour in the eggs and continue with the recipe.

12	large eggs	1	teaspoon dried thyme
¼	cup water	½	teaspoon salt
¾	lb. potatoes	¼	teaspoon freshly ground pepper
1	medium onion, sliced	2	garlic cloves, minced
1	red bell pepper, sliced	1	teaspoon salt
2	tablespoons olive oil	1	tablespoon chopped fresh parsley
2	tablespoons minced fresh rosemary		

1. In large bowl, whisk eggs with water until blended.

2. Scrub and peel potatoes. (If you are using new potatoes, there is no need to peel.) Cut into ⅛-inch slices or small cubes; cover with water in large pot. Cook potatoes over medium-high heat until fork-tender.

3. Heat oil in large skillet over medium heat. Sauté onions and bell pepper 5 minutes, stirring occasionally until onions start to brown.

4. Drain potatoes; pat dry. Add potatoes, rosemary, thyme, ½ of the teaspoon salt and onions to bell peppers; toss 5 minutes, stirring frequently. Cover skillet loosely; cook an additional 5 minutes, lifting cover to stir 3 or 4 times. Remove cover and sample 2 or 3 pieces of potato. If they are soft, add garlic; if not, continue to cook until softened. Toss vegetables with garlic and cook 2 to 3 minutes until garlic is fragrant.

5. Heat broiler. Stir remaining ½ teaspoon salt and 1 tablespoon chopped parsley into beaten eggs. Pour into skillet, spreading vegetables evenly. Reduce heat to low; cook eggs slowly. Run heat-resistant or thin wooden spatula around edge 2 or 3 times to loosen omelet from pan, allowing uncooked egg to spill over edge to bottom of skillet. Cook 10 minutes or until bottom and sides of omelet have set.

6. Place skillet under broiler, turning as necessary for even cooking. Broil about 4 minutes or until top of omelet is lightly browned and eggs are slightly puffy. Cut omelet into wedges. Garnish with additional parsley.

6 to 8 servings

Zucchinis Stuffed with Goat Cheese and Fresh Herbs

Serve this chilled stuffed zucchini on the plate with the Potato, Red Bell Pepper and Onion Frittata. Because the frittata is so hearty and full of vegetables, the zucchini is more like a garnish, not a full vegetable course. This recipe can easily be doubled if you want to serve each guest more than one.

⅔ cup (6 oz.) soft fresh goat cheese	1 tablespoon chopped fresh parsley
2 tablespoons milk or half-and-half	1 tablespoon chopped fresh basil
2 teaspoons sherry vinegar or other wine vinegar	2 tablespoons extra-virgin olive oil
	½ teaspoon salt
1 tablespoon unseasoned dry bread crumbs	1 teaspoon freshly ground pepper
	3 (5- to 7-inch) zucchini
1 teaspoon minced shallots or 2 teaspoons minced onion	2 tablespoons extra-virgin olive oil, plus more for drizzling
½ teaspoon chopped fresh thyme	

1. In small bowl, combine goat cheese, milk and vinegar with fork until smooth. Stir in bread crumbs, shallots, thyme, parsley, basil and oil. Season with salt and pepper. Cover and refrigerate filling several hours.

2. Rinse and scrub zucchinis; pat dry. Trim off ends; cut zucchini in half, lengthwise. Plane off bottoms to stabilize. Scoop out seeds, leaving as much vegetable flesh as possible. Blanch zucchini in unsalted simmering water 3 to 5 minutes or until just cooked but not soft. Rinse briefly under cold water; drain and cool.

3. One or two hours before serving, divide goat cheese mixture evenly among zucchini; cover and refrigerate. Just before serving, drizzle each piece with several drops extra-virgin olive oil; garnish with herb sprigs, if desired.

6 servings

Melon, Mozzarella and Tomato Salad

This fresh and easy summer salad combines sweet, tart and creamy flavors. Serve it in a large glass bowl to show off its bright colors.

1 cantaloupe	⅛ teaspoon freshly ground pepper
¾ lb. (about ¾ cup) mozzarella cut into 1-inch cubes, drained, dried	¼ cup extra-virgin olive oil
	2 tablespoons chopped fresh parsley
1 (16-oz.) pkg. cherry tomatoes, drained	2 tablespoons chopped fresh chives
	6 cups trimmed mesclun or watercress greens
2 tablespoons white wine vinegar	
½ teaspoon salt plus more to taste	

1. Remove seeds from cantaloupe.

2. Just before serving, combine melon, cheese and tomatoes in large bowl; toss with vinegar, salt, pepper, oil, parsley and chives.

3. Divide salad greens among 6 salad plates. Use additional vinegar, salt, pepper and oil to dress greens, if desired.

6 servings

Note:

Soft, moist and freshly made mozzarella is much better for this recipe than the firmer mass-produced mozzarella.

Melon, Mozzarella and Tomato Salad

Dessert Crepes with Peaches, Raspberry Puree and Orange-Flavored Liqueur Whipped Cream

CREPES

- 4 eggs
- 2 cups whole milk
- 1 to 1½ cups all-purpose flour
- 2 tablespoons sugar
- ¼ teaspoon salt
- 1 teaspoon vanilla
- 4 tablespoons vegetable oil or melted butter, plus more for cooking crepes

FILLING

- 2½ cups fresh raspberries or 1 (12- or 14-oz.) bag frozen unsweetened raspberries, thawed
- 6 tablespoons superfine sugar
- ½ cup fresh orange juice

TOPPING

- 1 cup heavy cream
- 2 tablespoons sugar
- 2 tablespoons orange-flavored liqueur

FRUIT

- 3 ripe peaches or nectarines, sliced
- 3 tablespoons orange-flavored liqueur
- 1 cup fresh raspberries
- ½ cup toasted slivered onions

For this cool summer dessert, make the crepes and raspberry puree in advance. An hour before serving, make the Orange-Flavored Liqueur Whipped Cream and slice the peaches. Then you'll be ready to assemble the dessert just before serving. The crepes do not need to be hot for this dessert; room temperature is fine. To make the dessert non-alcoholic, substitute orange juice for the orange-flavored liqueur.

1. To prepare crepes, lightly beat eggs in large bowl; stir in milk. In medium bowl, combine flour, sugar and salt; gradually whisk into egg mixture. Batter should be consistency of whipping cream. With whisk or electric mixer, beat batter 30 seconds to 1 minute or until smooth. Stir in vanilla. Refrigerate batter 30 to 60 minutes.

2. If you prefer, prepare crepe batter in blender or food processor. Combine eggs and milk in blender or food processor; process 2 or 3 seconds. In medium bowl, stir together flour, sugar and salt. Add to blender or food processor; process 5 to 10 seconds, stopping to scrape flour from sides, if necessary. Stir in vanilla. Refrigerate 30 to 60 minutes.

3. Remove batter from refrigerator; stir in oil. (If using melted butter, let batter warm up a few minutes so butter will not solidify.) Add more liquid if batter has become significantly thicker during resting period. Pass batter through strainer.

4. Use 2 to 3 tablespoons batter per crepe. Heat a few drops of oil in large skillet over medium-high heat until hot. Pour batter into pan, rotating pan to spread batter evenly. When batter is nearly dry and no longer shiny on top, use spatula to turn crepe. Briefly cook crepe on second side, just long enough to dry surface and create a few lightly browned spots. Stack crepes as they cool; refrigerate. (To freeze crepes, stack 4 cool crepes and top with 2 small squares parchment paper, then stack another 4 crepes. Repeat as necessary. Wrap crepes in plastic wrap and place in freezer bag. Thaw in refrigerator before using.)

5. To prepare filling, in blender or food processor, puree raspberries with sugar and orange juice. Pass puree through strainer to remove seeds; refrigerate.

6. To prepare topping, combine cream sugar and orange-flavored liqueur in large bowl; whip at medium speed until soft peaks form. Set aside.

7. Place peaches in large bowl. Add orange-flavored liqueur to peaches; toss.

8. Spoon 3 tablespoons puree on each of 6 serving plates. Place 2 crepes on each plate. Fold each crepe in half, and in half again, to make a small triangle. Spoon peaches and their juice around crepes and over triangle tips. Top with dollop of topping. Garnish with whole raspberries and almonds. Store in refrigerator.

28 crepes, 2 cups raspberry sauce

Dessert Crepes with Peaches, Raspberry Puree and Orange-Flavored Liqueur Whipped Cream

Sandwich Selections

by Lisa Golden Schroeder

Sometimes sandwiches just fit the mood and the occasion. Select from these ideas to make the meal a creative and delicious one.

Tuscan BLT

selections

Tuscan BLT

Peachy Barbecued Chicken Wraps with Roasted Corn Salsa

Baja Fish Tacos

Crab Rolls

These sandwich ideas—from a B.L.T. to tacos like you've never had before—start with tradition and take it to new taste levels.

Tuscan BLT

Look for vine-ripened tomatoes for this sun-kissed sandwich. A trip to a local farmers' market should yield bushels of tomatoes bursting with flavor, as well as huge bouquets of basil. Any herbed vinegar would be delightful for marinating the tomatoes.

3	ripe tomatoes, sliced	¼	teaspoon freshly ground pepper
2	tablespoons herbed red wine or sherry vinegar	1	(1-lb.) loaf foccacia
1	tablespoon olive oil	4	oz. smoked Provolone cheese, sliced
½	teaspoon kosher (coarse) salt	4	oz. prosciutto ham, thinly sliced
		12	large fresh basil leaves

1. Layer tomato slices in glass 9-inch pie plate. Sprinkle with vinegar, olive oil, salt and pepper. Let stand 15 minutes.

2. Slice bread in half horizontally. Layer tomatoes, cheese, loosely rolled prosciutto slices and basil leaves on bottom half of bread. Top with remaining loaf. Cut into wedges. Serve with honey Dijon mustard, if desired.

4 servings

Note:

Juicy wedges of summer melon and some berry shortcake can top off a great patio meal.

Peachy Barbecued Chicken Wraps with Roasted Corn Salsa

To play up the seasonal flavor of the peach-barbecue sauce on this chicken, try grilling fresh peaches. Halve, pit and brush cut sides with sauce. Place cutside down on grill and cook until browned and tender. Slice and wrap in tortillas with the chicken and sauce.

1	cup barbecue sauce	2	tablespoons olive oil
½	cup peach preserves	4	boneless skinless chicken breast halves
2	large ears of corn, husks and cornsilk removed*	2	to 3 tablespoons fresh lime juice
1	small red onion, sliced	2	pitted sliced ripe avocados
1	small green bell pepper, quartered lengthwise	8	(10-inch) warm flour tortillas

TIP:

*Corn may take longer to cook. Test kernel with tip of knife. If it's not tender, move to center of grill, cover, and cook an additional 8 to 10 minutes.

1. Heat grill.

2. In small bowl, combine barbecue sauce and preserves; mix well.

3. Lightly brush corn, onion and bell pepper with oil; place around edge of grill. Place chicken in center of gas grill over medium heat or on charcoal grill 4 to 6 inches from medium coals. Cover and cook 3 minutes. Turn chicken; brush with barbecue sauce. Cook an additional 3 minutes; turn again. Brush with barbecue sauce mixture. Cook 4 minutes or until chicken is no longer pink in center. Turn vegetables when turning chicken.

4. Remove chicken and vegetables from grill. Keep chicken warm. Slice corn kernels off cobs into a medium bowl. Chop onion and bell pepper; stir into corn with lime juice. Place remaining barbecue sauce in small saucepan and bring mixture to a boil over medium-high heat. Remove pan from heat and pour mixture into small bowl.

5. To serve, slice chicken. Place some chicken, corn salsa, avocado and warm barbecue sauce on tortillas. Fold up and serve.

4 servings

Note:

Try grilled boneless pork chops instead of the chicken. To warm the tortillas, wrap them in aluminum foil and place on the edge of the grill while the chicken is cooking.

Baja Fish Tacos

No need to head to Mexico to enjoy the Pacific flavors of grilled fish wrapped in warm tortillas, dripping with a tangy cilantro sauce and crisp cabbage slaw. Halibut, red snapper, rock cod or sea bass fillets would make good alternatives to tuna, as they are firm-fleshed and grill well.

Note:

For more zip in the cilantro sauce, use serrano chiles instead of jalapeños. Serranos are smaller, but they pack more punch! For a creamy cilantro sauce, stir in ¼ cup sour cream.

SLAW
- 2½ cups finely shredded red cabbage
- ⅓ cup thinly sliced red onion
- 3 tablespoons seasoned rice vinegar
- 1 tablespoon olive oil
- ¼ teaspoon salt

SAUCE
- 1 (3½- to 4-oz.) bunch fresh cilantro
- 1 small white onion, coarsely chopped

- ½ teaspoon cumin
- 1 to 2 jalapeño chiles, seeded, quartered
- 3 tablespoons fresh lime juice
- ½ teaspoon salt
- 2 teaspoons olive oil

- 1 lb. fresh tuna steak
- 8 warm corn tortillas

1. Heat grill.

2. In medium bowl, combine cabbage, onion, vinegar, oil and salt; set aside.

3. Clean cilantro and trim bottoms of stems (leave upper stems intact). In blender, combine cilantro, onion, cumin seeds, chiles, lime juice and salt; blend until smooth. Reserve ¼ cup of the cilantro sauce. Stir in 2 teaspoons oil; set aside. Refrigerate remaining sauce until serving time.

4. Brush fish with reserved cilantro-oil mixture. Place fish on gas grill over medium-high heat or on charcoal grill 4 to 6 inches over medium coals. Cover and cook, turning once and brushing with sauce, about 10 minutes or until fish flakes easily with fork. Discard any remaining brushing sauce.

5. Assemble tacos by placing grilled fish on warm tortilla. Top with cabbage slaw and drizzle with cilantro sauce. Fold over and serve.

4 servings

Crab Rolls

You could make this fresh and easy seafood salad with some bay shrimp, or stuff it into avocado halves. Here, used as a filling for soft sandwich rolls, a light summer salad becomes portable ... or perfect for waterside entertaining.

- ⅓ cup reduced-fat mayonnaise
- ⅓ cup buttermilk
- 2 tablespoons minced fresh parsley
- 1 tablespoon chopped fresh dill or 1 teaspoon dried
- 2 teaspoons grated lemon peel
- ¼ teaspoon freshly ground pepper

- 8 oz. cooked crabmeat
- ½ cup diced celery
- ¼ cup sliced green onion
- 4 large, soft sandwich rolls
- 4 slices tomato
- 4 arugula leaves

1. In large bowl, combine mayonnaise, buttermilk, parsley, dill, lemon peel and pepper; stir until smooth. Stir in crab, celery and onion; mix well.

2. Fill sandwich rolls with crab salad, sliced tomato and lettuce.

4 servings

Baja Fish Tacos

Crab Rolls

Lobster on the GRILL

by Janice Cole, Holly Herrick,
Lisa Golden Schroeder
and Charla Draper

*You can grill almost any meat
or seafood, and lobster
is no exception.
Here's how to do it up right.
We've included all the
necessary side dishes too.*

Grilled Lobster with Shallot-Red Pepper Butter

menu

Grilled Lobster with Shallot-Red Pepper Butter

Tomato and Asparagus Salad

Basil-Tomato Corn Muffins

Chocolate Berry Cobbler

A meal with lobster is always a special occasion. Lead in with Tomato and Asparagus Salad, add great Basil-Tomato Corn Muffins, then finish with a Chocolate Berry Cobbler.

Grilled Lobster with Shallot-Red Pepper Butter

The smokiness of lobster off the grill will become a new favorite technique. Remember these three important facts about cooking lobster: select an active lobster; always cook lobster while it's alive; and never store lobster on ice or hold them in fresh (tap) water.

BUTTER
1 cup butter
½ cup finely chopped shallots
¼ cup fresh lemon juice
2 teaspoons crushed
    red pepper

LOBSTER
4 quarts (16 cups) water
¼ cup sea salt
4 (1¼ to 1½ lb.) lobsters

1. Melt butter in small saucepan over medium heat. Add shallots; sauté 60 to 90 seconds or until shallots are fragrant and begin to soften. Stir in lemon juice and pepper; remove from heat. Divide butter mixture in half. Set aside half of mixture to brush on lobster during grilling; reserve remaining half to serve warm with lobster.

2. Place water and salt in large pot. Cover; bring to a boil over high heat. Add lobsters; cover and return to a boil. When water boils, cook lobsters 3 to 4 minutes or until lobster shells begin to turn a mottled red. Remove lobsters from pot; immediately plunge into large bowl of ice water to stop cooking.

3. Place lobsters on cutting board; cut in half lengthwise. Remove sand sac, intestinal track and liver. Crack claws to allow heat from grill to penetrate. (Lobster can be made up to 3 hours ahead. Cover and refrigerate.)

4. Heat grill. Brush lobster halves with half of butter mixture. Place on gas grill over medium heat or on charcoal grill 4 to 6 inches from hot coals. Cook 6 to 8 minutes or until lobster meat is opaque, turning once and brushing occasionally with butter mixture. Heat remaining butter mixture in small saucepan until warm. Serve lobsters with warm butter mixture.

4 servings

Tomato and Asparagus Salad

This luscious salad showcases the produce from any garden or market. Serve at room temperature.

1 lb. asparagus, trimmed
3 large red tomatoes, thinly sliced
8 oz. yellow or red cherry tomatoes, halved vertically
3 tablespoons extra-virgin olive oil

4 teaspoons red wine vinegar
¼ cup chopped fresh basil
⅛ teaspoon kosher (coarse) salt
¼ teaspoon freshly ground pepper

1. Cook asparagus in boiling salted water 3 to 5 minutes or until crisp-tender. Immediately drain and submerge asparagus in very cold water.* When cool, drain and pat dry.

2. To serve, arrange tomato slices in center of serving platter. Sprinkle cherry tomatoes over top; fan asparagus spears around edge of platter. Drizzle with oil and vinegar. Sprinkle with basil, salt and pepper.

6 servings

TIP:

*This important step, called "refreshing," preserves the brilliant green color of the asparagus.

Basil-Tomato Corn Muffins

The combination of fresh corn and sun-dried tomatoes gives a wonderful natural sweetness to the muffins.

1 cup cornmeal	¼ cup butter, melted
1 cup all-purpose flour	2 cups corn
2 tablespoons sugar	½ cup chopped, oil-packed sun-dried
4 teaspoons baking powder	tomatoes, drained
¾ teaspoon salt	2 tablespoons finely chopped fresh
1 cup milk	basil
2 eggs	

1. Heat oven to 400°F. Grease 12 muffin cups. In large bowl, combine cornmeal, flour, sugar, baking powder and salt; mix well.

2. In small bowl, combine milk and eggs; beat at medium speed until frothy. Add milk mixture and butter to flour mixture; stir just until moistened. Fold in corn, tomatoes and basil. Spoon batter evenly into muffin cups.

3. Bake 20 to 25 minutes or until toothpick inserted near center comes out clean. Serve warm.

12 muffins

Chocolate Berry Cobbler

This chocolate cobbler tastes just like a warm, moist chocolate brownie, nicely complemented with fresh fruit.

2 cups fresh blueberries	¼ teaspoon salt
2 cups fresh raspberries	¼ cup unsalted butter, chilled, cut up
2 cups sliced fresh strawberries	⅓ cup buttermilk
1¼ cups plus 1 tablespoon sugar	1 egg
1 cup plus 2 tablespoons	
all-purpose flour	**TOPPING**
¼ cup unsweetened	½ cup whipping cream
Dutch-process cocoa	1 tablespoon sugar
½ teaspoon baking soda	

1. Heat oven to 425°F. Spray 9-inch square pan with nonstick cooking spray. In large bowl, combine berries, ½ cup of the sugar and 2 tablespoons of the flour; mix gently. Spoon into pan.

2. In medium bowl, combine remaining 1 cup flour, cocoa, ¾ cup of the sugar, baking soda and salt; mix well. With pastry blender or 2 knives, cut in butter until mixture crumbles. In small bowl, combine buttermilk and egg; blend well. Stir egg mixture into flour mixture until well blended.

3. Drop dough by spoonfuls over berry mixture. Sprinkle with remaining 1 tablespoon of sugar.

4. Bake 25 to 35 minutes or until fruit is bubbly and cobbler is set. (Top surface should be dull and dry to the touch.)

5. Meanwhile, in small bowl, whip cream with 1 tablespoon sugar until soft peaks form. Cover; refrigerate. Serve warm cobbler with whipped cream.

6 servings

Basil-Tomato Corn Muffins

Chocolate Berry Cobbler

Index